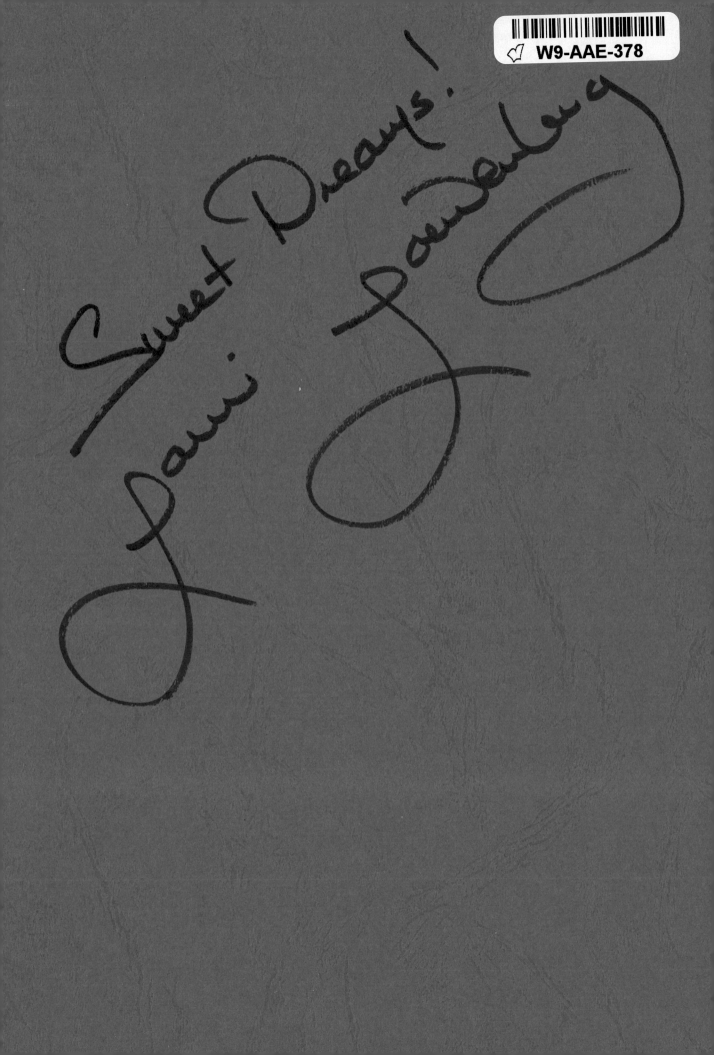

Acknowledgements

ಖ೦೮ಜ೭೦೧

First and foremost, I want to thank God for blessing each and every one of us with these wierd, wonderful jewels of wisdom each and every night. I want to thank my strikingly handsome husband for being my support, my cheer leader, my guidance counselor and my biggest fan. I love you! Thank you, thank you Dr. Katia Romanoff for teaching me, mentoring me, writing with me, befriending me and inspiring me. I want to thank my dear friends Rachael Hamilton and Brett Lurman for making sure my I's were crossed and my T's were dotted. Oops! See how important you are? Thank you to my brother Michael Quinn, my dear, dear friend Nicole Belenfante, and Bob Branch - the most talented web master in the world, for contributing their wonderful art to this book. Thank you to all the editors of all the publications that run The Dream Zone column. Thank you to all the dreamers that have contributed a little piece of their psyche to this book. Thank you to all the program directors, morning show producers and DJs that have had me on their shows and let me run my big yapper! And thank you to all my readers. I appreciate you picking up this book and allowing me to teach you a little something; something I hope will enrich your lives and that you will always carry with you.

Copyright © 2007 by The Dream Zone Companies, Inc.

ISBN: 0-615-12384-8

FOREWORD

By Katia Romanoff, Ph.D.

ೞഠೞ൮

You're going to love this book! It's not a how-to book, yet you'll come away with an ancient wisdom, an ancestral wisdom that will change your life.

Like it or not, we spend one third of our lives in the dream state. Something is going on in there! Even nightmares have a personal message that we should heed. What realms and knowledge do we contact while dreaming? What is this force that moves within our minds and souls and sends us these strange images and symbols? Why not tap into this totally free resource and make use of one third of your time? In my years of private practice helping people understand their lives thru dreams, I have seen so many success stories. Dreams are a vital part of our lives and it's a waste to ignore them. No matter how nonsensical, bizarre, weird or frightful your dreams seem, there is a meaning there custom made for you and your life *right now*.

Symbols and elements in your dreams can seem goofy and often disturbing. Lauri helps you contact the power reserves behind your dream symbols and use them to energize your life. The chapters in this book put your inner reserves, your "secret power" to work for *you*. Everything from dark fears, silly desires, to intense desires and the hidden workings of your relationships will suddenly make sense. The people around you will notice the change in you, and they can't help but benefit from your new access to wisdom.

Everything in this book, the artwork, the dream samples, the fascinating topics discussed, will access a force you may not know, which nonetheless is moving within you this minute. It comes from a source you also may not be aware of, that moves thruout the universe positively guiding and enlightening minds and lives.

Re-vitalize your personality, your understanding of the cosmos and of your personal life — just by taking a look at this book. Open your mind and get to know your dreamweaver, learn Lauri's insightful methods to decipher these made-just-for-you messages.

What are *your* dreams trying to tell *you*? You're about to find out....

Table of Contents

ഇഗ3ജ്ഇ൨

"Dreams are the road to the royal unconscious." - Sigmund Freud
Artist: Lauri Quinn Loewenberg **Medium:** Color pencil/DSigital media

Chapter One
What are Dreams?

ಖಁಊಟ಼ಖಂಟಌ

"I had the WEIRDEST dream last night…" How many times have you heard yourself saying those words? We've all had our share of dreams that linger among our thoughts for days. Some dreams leave us filled with a sense of awe. Some dreams cause us great fear or concern. And some dreams can even make us ask ourselves, "Why the HECK would I dream something so bizarre?! Did that really come from my head?"

Mankind has been intrigued by the mysteries of the dreaming mind for thousands of years. The ancient Romans built temples for the sole purpose of dream incubation and ancient people even traveled great distances to spend a night in these "dream temples" in hopes of receiving a dream of healing or enlightenment. Native Americans believed that dreams were messages of guidance from The Great Spirit. Dreams hold a prominent place in The Bible as well, as there are over seven hundred references to dreams and visions within its pages.

What ARE dreams? Why do we dream? And why should we give them any relevance in our lives? Well, dreams actually serve two major purposes, a physiological purpose and a psychological purpose.

Physiologically, dreaming is a natural and necessary function of the brain. We all dream. Anyone who says they don't is mistaken; he or she simply isn't remembering them. During sleep, the brain goes through many stages of brain wave patterns.

The first stage is the "Alpha" stage. During this stage our brain waves begin to slow down to anywhere from eight to fourteen cycles per second. This is actually a meditative state also known as the "Hypnagogic" state. Here, we're not quite asleep nor fully awake. This is when the mind will play tricks and we might think we see some strange man standing in the corner, feel a "ghost" sit down on the bed, or even think we are leaving our bodies. The right-brain and the left-brain are equals at this point and allow us to tap into the depths of our creative pool, compose a beautiful symphony, find the solution to a nagging problem and even come up with the world's greatest invention! At this stage our brain waves are at the "genius" level where our thinking is not unlike that of Einstein or Edison.

The second stage of sleep is the "Theta" stage. During this stage our brain waves slow down even more, about four to seven cycles per second. In this stage there are some vague dreams and thoughts occurring. Scientists call this the non- rapid eye movement (N-REM) stage.

Third is the "Delta" stage of sleep. Brain waves are now about five-tenths to three and five-tenths of a cycle per second. This is deep sleep where the body rejuvenates itself. The Delta stage is when we get our "beauty rest" A lack of deep sleep actually ages the body! After the "Delta" stage we zip back up to the "Alpha" stage again and this is when we begin to dream. When we dream we are in REM sleep. It is called REM because our eyes are actually rapidly moving about underneath those closed lids. We are actually watching what is going on in our dream! It is also believed that all that eye movement helps to supply much-needed oxygen to the cornea of the eye.

The brain goes through these various stages of sleep every ninety minutes throughout the night until we wake up. And each time we enter the "Alpha" stage our time spent dreaming is longer and longer. That last dream we have before we wake up could have been up to forty-five minutes long!

All these stages of sleep, especially the REM stage, are believed to play a part in the learning process.

₨☥♒₧

Psychologically, dreams are the language of the subconscious. The subconscious mind uses dreams as a means of relaying messages to us. The subconscious mind is always working. When we're awake it stays *sub*-merged, below the surface, keeping quiet but observing everything. As we go about our lives, it grabs every thought, emotion and sensation we ever experience and

stores it away for future use. That is why our dreams often seem so real. Unlike our conscious mind, it has no prejudices and it is not critical. It is honest, pure and untainted. So, when we go to sleep each night and our conscious mind slips away, our subconscious mind rises to the top and begins to play!

Our subconscious will place us in all sorts of scenarios accompanied by unusual characters and objects. One night we may find ourselves driving down a country road in a convertible with a whale in the backseat enjoying the ride, and the next night we may find ourselves in the middle of the ocean floating on a giant pickle! No matter how absurd these scenarios may seem they are actually reflections of our daily lives… or at least how our ssubconscious sees it, anyway.

"Okay, so how in the world does floating on a giant pickle have anything to do with my life," you might ask? Well first of all, it's important to remember that the subconscious mind does not think in literal terms like our conscious mind. It thinks in symbolic terms, in metaphors. For example, if you are in a tough situation that is causing you to feel isolated in your waking life, then to your subconscious mind, you are essentially "in a pickle" way out in the middle of nowhere. So, now you are able to see your situation in a different light, and even though it's a ridiculous scenario, your situation may suddenly become much clearer to you now. From this particular dream you may realize that the only person that can get you out of this mess… is YOU!

These strange little scenarios we call dreams are given to us each night so that we can learn from them, and see our lives and the world around us from a much wiser point of view. Our dreams are our very own tools for self-discovery and self-improvement. And if only we'd pay closer attention to this enlightened part of ourselves, we'd all live happier, more fulfilling lives.

ജഇൠഏ

"*Whether we find ourselves in a car plunging down a steep slope, or piloting a plane through the heavenly skies, we will do well to ask why our unconscious put us there.*" - the Talmud

Artist: Lauri Quinn Loewenberg   **Medium:** Digital media

Chapter Two
Fleeing, Falling, Flying…
The Most Common
Dream Themes

ɛᎾᏨᏜᏇᏇ

"Fleeing from a Man in a Fuzzy Hat"

I am in my front yard watering my Gladiolas. I notice that there are little white bugs all over the blossoms. As I take a closer look at the little critters, I hear a rustling behind me. I turn around to find a very large man wearing a giant fuzzy hat. A sense of fear comes over me and I take off, running as fast as I can. I run through the neighborhood, screaming for help. I can hear the man's footsteps right behind me. They are getting closer and closer. I feel his heavy hand on my shoulder and… I wake up with my heart racing and sweat trickling down my face.

Whew! Boy, was I glad to wake up from THAT dream! **Fleeing** is one of the most common themes that show up in our dreams. It is caused by anxiety over something we are trying to avoid, something we are symbolically "running from."

My dream was the result of anxiety I was having over my relationship with my brother-in-law. In the beginning, there was an enormous lack of communication between us, mainly due to my inability to speak up. I allowed little things to "bug me." My dream was showing me that there was "fertile ground" for a beautiful relationship to "blossom" if I would just get all those little annoyances out of the way. For many years I would "run from" the confrontation that he and I needed to have that would allow us to work out our issues. The only thing I gained from this constant avoidance was a seemingly endless barrage of mysterious dream characters hot on my heels.

It is always important to take a good look at what or who is chasing us in our "fleeing dreams." It will usually give us clues as to what role we play in the situation. In my dream, I was being chased by a very large man wearing a fuzzy hat. The large scale of my pursuer reflects what a big problem this had become, while the fuzzy hat symbolized the way I covered and protected my thoughts just as a hat covers and protects the head.

After repeatedly getting this dream in various forms, I finally had a heart to heart discussion my brother-in-law about our relationship and all the little things that bugged us about the other. Ever since, our relationship has continued to blossom and I am no longer tortured by large men in fuzzy hats!

Here is another good example of how our dreams can show us what it is we are trying to avoid in waking life.

"Fleeing from a Giant Tube of Lipstick"

I dreamed my ex-best friend was throwing makeup at me. The funny and kinda scary thing was that the lipstick she threw became as big as I am and then chased after me! I woke up before it could get me. – Shelly 19, Memphis, Tennessee

Okay, so maybe a giant tube of lipstick isn't quite as scary as a large man in a fuzzy hat, but it certainly got Shelly's attention. And her pursuer still gives us very good clues as to the role Shelly was playing in her situation at that time. In her dream, she was running from make-up. In waking life, she was trying to avoid making up with her friend. What's more, the particular piece of make-up she was running from was a tube of lipstick. Lipstick draws attention to one's mouth and one uses the mouth to say the words, "I'm sorry."

Deep down, Shelly knew she wanted to make up with her friend but she didn't want to be the one to make the first move. Her dream not only showed her that this was something she should stop avoiding, but that her friend was wanting to make up as well. After all, her friend was the one throwing the make-up in the first place! In waking life, her friend was throwing hints that she wanted their feud to end.

So the next time you find yourself trying to escape from a mysterious man in black, a gang of thugs or even an oversized cosmetic, know that it is a call from your subconscious mind to STOP RUNNING from the issue. Face the person or the problem head on and you'll soon find the only thing behind you now is your anxiety.

Falling

Falling is another common dream theme we all get. Whether we're in a plane that's taking a nose dive, in a car driving off a cliff or just in our own bodies, from time to time we all find ourselves plummeting through the air, going down, down, down…

Falling is very real at the time and we are usually in free-fall long enough to realize there's nothing we can do about it. That realization is usually the core to these less than pleasant dreams; in our waking lives we've realized that we have lost control of something, a relationship, our career, etc. The loss of control can lead to feelings of failure, disappointment or a fear that we have lost status. From all of these feelings, the falling dream will emerge.

"Falling Building"

I dreamed I was in my childhood bedroom with my best childhood friend. The room began to shake violently. We were having an earthquake. I looked out the window and saw that we were actually on the top floor of a skyscraper. Suddenly, I felt the room tilt to the side and the building we were in began to fall. As we, along with all the furniture, were sliding down the floor I was yelling, "It's going to be okay! Just hang on! We're going to be okay!" That's when I woke up. – Barb 30, Greenville, South Carolina

At the time of this dream, Barb had just taken a job as the manager of a toy store. What she thought would be a fun and fairly easy job turned out to be more stressful and difficult than she anticipated. The childhood bedroom and friend are both symbolic of the environment she thought she would be working in. The skyscraper reflects her "high" hopes for this job, not to mention how high she "built" herself up to her boss in order to get the job. Two weeks into the job she nearly had a nervous breakdown (hence the earthquake) and all her hopes and ideals came crashing down, leaving her with a sense of failure, disappointment and the fear of being demoted.

But Barb's dream also offers encouragement, as most of our dreams do. As the building she was in began to fall, Barb kept telling herself, "It's going to be okay, just hang on." This advice she was giving herself came from her intuition, her wiser self. And what good advice it was! We should all learn from Barb's dream to just hang in there, because no matter how difficult a situation may be, things will eventually get better.

Flying and Floating

On the opposite end of the dream spectrum are the flying and floating dreams. These dreams allow us to soar through the air like a jet plane with the wind whipping through our hair (and the occasional bug in our teeth). To experience weightlessness and to master a feat beyond human capability gives one a sense of power and control. This is why flying and floating dreams will often come to us – to empower us to "rise above" our earthbound woes and "soar to new heights."

"Flying Instead of Dying"

I was riding with a group of people on the back of a truck filled with the most beautiful, bright red tomatoes. I love tomatoes and could not resist eating one. As soon as I ate one I was arrested because the tomatoes in this land were sacred! The punishment for eating a tomato was death. I asked if I could choose how I would die. They said, "Yes." I said, "Take me to your highest building and push me out the window." They did this and when they did, I took off and flew away like a bird. Somehow I knew I could fly. - Joyce 57, Midlothian, Virginia

Joyce's dream reflects her feelings of being overburdened (the overloaded truck) and oppressed (being arrested for eating a tomato). As she is falling to her death (her desire to "kill off" this part of her life), she suddenly flies away like a bird. This is the way her mind reassures her that she has the ability within her to free herself from her earthly woes. She *can* rise above and beyond the things that weigh down her spirit.

Sometimes flying dreams simply mirror our state of mind. When we feel something in our life, such as our career, a relationship, or even our self-esteem, is "reaching new heights" we can get a flying dream. I like to look at it as a pat on the back from the subconscious. It's as if it is saying to us, "You've been doing a pretty good job lately. I'm proud of you. Here ya go… have a flying dream!"

"Flying Along the Freeway"

My husband and I are flying along the freeway just above all the traffic. Our arms are stretched out to either side as if we were airplanes. We are going very fast! The theme to "The Lone Ranger" is playing. I'm having such a great time that I wake myself up laughing!
- Camille 24, Las Vegas, Nevada

Camille had this dream on the night of her and her husband's first wedding anniversary. Camille is clearly very happy in her marriage and excited about what the future holds for her and hubby, which is why her dreaming mind had her flying along the freeway. Freeways symbolize the road of life. At the time of this dream, Camille felt that she and her husband could "rise above" the ordinary (the traffic) and continue to "soar to new heights."

But there are occasions when being lighter than air can be a hindrance rather than a "high," such as when we're having trouble getting "grounded."

"Floating in Bed"

I have this recurring dream that I wake up and am floating a foot or two above my bed and have a hard time getting down. I'll grab on to the headboard and try to pull myself down but am never able to. I'll also dream of being at work or the store or whatever and am floating a foot or two off the ground. I'm very embarrassed because I know people are staring.
-   Jenna 28, Buffalo, New York

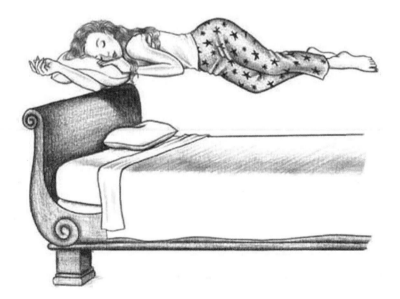

Jenna's dream was recurring, which means it was commenting on an ongoing issue. Jenna was having a hard time keeping a job. She didn't know what she wanted to do with her life and couldn't find anything that made her happy. All this instability made her subconscious mind feel as though she were suspended in mid-air, unable to gain footing. Once Jenna was able to find a job she could stick to, these dreams stopped.

The next time you get a flying or floating dream, pay attention to how you are behaving in the air. Are you in control, soaring like a bird and enjoying the freedom, or are you barely able to get off the ground? The details are important because they are good indications as to how those "high" goals you've set for yourself are coming along.

ೞಚಿೞೱಠ

"In sleep we have the naked and natural thoughts of our souls…" – Owen Feltham

Artist: Lauri Quinn Loewenberg **Medium:** Color pencil/Digital media

Chapter Three

Naked as a Jay Bird

ഇൽ൭ഇ

"Nowhere to Get Dressed"

I am walking up the stairs to the playroom. When I reach the top, I find several people I don't know playing Billiards. I suddenly realize I don't have one stitch of clothing on. I say to my guests, "Please excuse me while I go find some clothes." I grab a pillow off the sofa to cover myself and run back downstairs to my bedroom. I open my bedroom door only to find an older woman whom I don't know. She tells me that she loves my hair. I thank her, politely grab a dress and excuse myself as I back out the door. I turn around and to my dismay; discover even more people I don't know in my living room. Anxiety rising, I trot through the living room as quickly as I can hoping no one will notice me before I make it to the bathroom. At last, I have reached my precious, private bathroom. I open the door, step inside and... BONK! I hit my head on the light fixture. My bathroom has shrunk and is so small I have no room to move. Sheesh!

Ah, the good ol' naked-in-public dream. How many times have you had THAT one? Standing there in all your glory for the whole world to see is a rather uncomfortable and embarrassing feeling for sure, and it makes you feel vulnerable and exposed… all eyes on you. Hellooo insecurity!! Not surprisingly, it is those very feelings in waking life that are often the cause of the dreaded naked-in-public dream.

At the time I had the aforementioned dream, I had just done my very first radio interview and was feeling very insecure about how it went. In the beginning of my dream I am walking UP the stairs, which symbolizes progress. Radio interviews were certainly a "step up" in my career. Once I discovered the unfamiliar people in my house I also discovered my lack of clothing, suggesting that I felt very vulnerable in front of that large, unfamiliar radio audience. The woman in my bedroom who complimented my hair was actually a bit of encouragement from my subconscious. Hair symbolizes one's thoughts and ideas because, like hair, thoughts and ideas sprout from the head. My dream was trying to show me that people were interested in my knowledge of dreams, which is also why this little interaction took place in a bedroom – where we sleep and dream. And as for the shrinking bathroom, well, that was a tough one for me to figure out. Looking back, I think it was my dreaming mind trying to discourage me from hiding. As frightening as my first radio interview was, deep down I knew it was something I needed to continue to do.

"Naked in Class"

I dreamt I was back in junior high. It was between classes and I couldn't figure out what class I was supposed to go to. Somebody grabbed me and pushed me into a classroom and said, "Here ya go!" Everyone in the classroom was looking at me funny. I looked down and saw that I was naked.
- Pam 28, Wakefield, Massachusetts

To dream of baring our birthday suit in public can also be the way our subconscious tries to show us we are unprepared to cope with a particular situation. Pam had this dream a couple of nights before she was going to start a new job selling stereos at a very busy electronics store. She didn't feel she had been properly trained and wasn't even sure why she had been hired. Being back in school really stood out to Pam, so she took that as a prodding from her dream to educate herself in her new field.

"Enjoying My Nudity"

How we feel about our nudity in our dreams greatly affects the meaning. Most often, finding our selves buck naked in front of others causes feelings of insecurity and embarrassment. Some of us, however, have the opposite response:

I dreamed I was having a party. I was sitting on the sofa talking to some guy. Well, I was naked and his armpit was smoking, kind of like a cigarette. I was very relaxed and it all seemed perfectly normal!
- Maria 27, Memphis, Tennessee

Maria certainly knows how to throw a party! And since this is her party, her dream shows that she knows how to be in control and comfortable in social situations. Her comfort with her nudity means Maria is the type of person who has nothing to hide. All good qualities to have! But there is a warning here as well… The man on the sofa, who seems to have a rather unique talent, is her masculine, assertive side (in dreams, members of the opposite sex will usually symbolize our masculine or feminine side). Armpits and smoking are both things that can be offensive. Maria's dream is telling her that her openness and assertiveness could rub some people the wrong way.

"Stripping"

I walked into a pub, took off all my clothes and left them on the bar. Then I lay down on the floor, totally naked, and put a large pillow on top of me and just meditated while everyone stared. – Peggy 27, Austin, Texas

At the time of this dream, Peggy had just started a job at a newspaper and was ready to focus and take her career seriously. Unfortunately, she was known to those around her as quirky and funny. Her dream reflects her desire to "strip away" those preconceived attitudes and ideas people had about her. She wanted everyone to see that she was now "grounded" and focused, hence the act of lying on the floor and meditating. The pillow shows us that this is a role in which she is "comfortable." And the last I heard, Peggy is still with the newspaper, newly married and doing quite well!

"Stripping Grandma"

I dreamed I walked into a strip club to find my grandmother up on the stage twirling about on the pole! She was as surprised to see me as I was to see her. I woke up shocked and disgusted. - Jeff 30, Buffalo, New York

Jeff's grandmother is not playing herself in this dream - thankfully! She is playing the part of Jeff's old fashioned and out dated views of women. Jeff strongly felt that the woman's place was in the home, raising the children and caring for the man. This attitude was actually making it difficult for him to sustain any lasting relationships. So Jeff's dreaming mind decided to shock him into attention by giving him this dream. It is telling him that he needs to "strip" away those old fashioned modes of thinking, which were the norm in his grandmother's time. But Jeff didn't want to drop his attitude just as much as he didn't want to see Granny drop her drawers. So his dream is letting him know that his attitude is as out of place in this day and age as Grandma is doing a table dance!

15

Naked-in-public dreams don't necessarily mean that the dreamer is the one de-frocked. Sometimes, everyone else is naked:

I was at a pool with my ex-husband and all the friends we had when we were married. All the girls but me were in the pool and topless. They were trying to get me to take my top off and jump in with them. I wanted to but I just didn't feel I looked as nice as they did.
– Lynnette 35, Peduca, Kentucky

In waking life, Lynette had to give up the circle of friends she and her ex-husband shared. She had this dream shortly after re-establishing contact with one of the girls in the circle. Lynette wanted very much to "dive" back in to these old friendships but she was feeling insecure about running into her ex, and she didn't know if her presence would cause problems or not. In her dream, her friends were urging her to take her top off and join them. This was her dreaming mind's way of urging her to "get something off her chest."

Because of this dream, Lynette decided it would be best if she told her ex what she wanted in hopes that they could come to an understanding that these were her friends, too.

"Naked Strangers"

If the naked individual in your dream is not someone you know then he or she will represent a part of your personality or a part of your life where you are feeling vulnerable, exposed or insecure:

I was trapped in an elevator with two strange people. One was a man with nothing but a clown nose on and he was holding a briefcase over his genitals. The other one was a nun in a very tiny mini- skirt. She was flirting with the man with the briefcase. I was not only trapped in the elevator but I was in between the two of them. – Darrell 24, Richmond, Virginia

The briefcase lets us know that the naked man in Darrell's dream symbolizes his work. Shortly before having this dream Darrell applied for a position as a supervisor. Expecting that he would get it, he began goofing off at his current position, hence the clown nose. Clearly, Darrell was not feeling insecure or vulnerable at work so his dream was letting him know he *should* be. His dreaming mind also trapped him in an elevator to let him know he was not going anywhere just yet so he better straighten up. As for the hot to trot Sister in the mini-skirt, she symbolizes another area of Darrell's life where he'd been feeling stuck – the available-for-romance department! His dating "habits" and desires conflicted with his moral beliefs, which caused him to constantly question himself and his relationships.

"Naked Man in the Grocery Store"

I dreamed I was in the grocery store in the cheese department. I don't know what kind of cheese I was looking for but all they had was Provolone. I looked up and saw a large, hairy, naked man standing there. I went to complain about it but everyone thought I was crazy for being bothered by this! - Jennifer 34, Silver Springs, Maryland

There's never anything exciting in this cheese department!

The grocery store represents Jennifer's storehouse of inner strengths, talents and abilities. The cheese she is searching for is some special tool she needs to accomplish her goal of managing the Italian restaurant where she has been working for several years. In her dream, she doesn't know what kind of cheese she's searching for because in waking life, she's not sure exactly what she needs to do in order to reach that managerial role. Notice how there was only Provolone available in her dream. Provolone is an Italian cheese and therefore symbolizes her work. The lack of any other cheese indicates Jennifer is not displaying enough variety of her own talents in her place of work. The naked, hairy guy is Jenneifer's "raw," masculine energy, that part of her that is assertive and takes action. Her dreaming mind is urging her to notice this aspect of her personality and "reveal" it to those around her at work. Yet, Jennifer is uncomfortable with this "untamed" part of her self, which is why she complained about it in the dream. Her dream is showing her that it is there within her mental storehouse and is there for the taking. Basically, Jennifer's gotta quit repressing her inner naked, hairy guy and let him out for the world to see!

The next time you bare your shiny hiny in a dream, pay attention to how it makes you feel. Were you embarrassed and uncomfortable? Were you proud or unconcerned? In what area of your life do you feel similar to the way you felt in your dream? Ask yourself if there's some attitude or behavior you need to "strip away." Maybe there's something you need to "reveal," or perhaps you've revealed too much. Just keep digging, sooner or later you'll be able to get to the "bare facts!"

ಸಚಿತ್ರ

"Dreams show us how to find a meaning in our lives, how to fulfill our own destiny, how to realize the greater potential of life within us." - Marie-Louise von Franz

Artist: Lauri Quinn Loewenberg   **Medium:** Digital Media

Chapter Four

Lost and Found

ౠ౧౿౪౷

"Losing My Purse"

I am at a bus station with Mary Tyler Moore. We are waiting for the bus to show up when I realize I have lost my purse. Mary thinks I may have left it in the bathroom. We rush into the bathroom and fling the doors to the stalls open, hoping to find the purse before the bus comes. Luckily, Mary finds the purse in the very last stall. As I reach to get it, it turns into a butterfly and flies out the door into the sky. I become very sad and wonder if it will come back.

I was practically in tears when I awoke from that dream. It seems kind of silly to think that one's purse turning into a butterfly and flying away would evoke such sadness, but to my subconscious the loss was very real and very significant.

At the time of this dream, my writing partner, Dr. Katia Romanoff and I were preparing to visit a newspaper convention in Memphis to promote "The Dream Zone" column. I had very high hopes for it, and if all went well, would make a career of it. So the career oriented, *"You're gonna make it after all"* gal we all know and love – Mary Tyler Moore - was my companion and helper in this dream. Together, we were waiting to catch a bus – waiting to catch an opportunity that would take us places. Before the bus arrived, I noticed I had lost my purse. Purses symbolize identity, values and credibility, as that is where we keep our I.D., money and credit cards (for men, the wallet will symbolize these things). Deep down, I was questioning my own credibility. Would the public identify with my column? The go-getter, Mary Tyler Moore part of me led me to my purse, which was in the bathroom, the place of cleansing. Yes, I needed to cleanse myself of these insecurities, believe in who I am and what I have to offer and catch that bus of opportunity! But before I could grab my purse it turned into a butterfly and flew away. My idea of who I am was transforming. Butterflies, one of my favorite dream symbols, signify a transformation into a higher form. My dream was encouraging me to break free from my "cocoon" of doubt and insecurity because the sky was the limit. I grew very sad because I knew I had to say good-bye to the old me, the girl who was too concerned of others' opinions to go out there and make something happen. I had to say good-bye to the girl I was comfortable being.

The loss of something in a dream is a call from our subconscious mind to question the permanency of things around or within us in waking life. In my dream, the loss was encouraging and positive; I certainly didn't want to be meek and insecure permanently! However, sometimes the loss can be a warning:

"Lost Shoes"

I was downtown trying to cross a busy street. I had lost my shoes and felt I could find them on the other side of the street. The cars were speeding by so fast I was having a hard time getting there. Then I looked down and noticed I was only wearing a slip. Not only had I lost my shoes but I had forgotten to finish getting dressed! - Betsy 75, Macon, Georgia

Dreaming of losing personal items is a common occurrence for the aging adult, as it reflects the loss of mobility, mental clarity and independence. Betsy was a very active seventy-five-year-old. She did lots of volunteering, loved to work in her garden and insisted on mowing her own yard. Unfortunately, her arthritis and a recent hip injury were forcing her to slow down. However, Betsy continued to fight and deny her ailments. Losing her shoes was the way Betsy's subconscious saw her loss of mobility, as our shoes help us to tread about comfortably. The speeding cars in her dream were not only letting Betsy know she was slowing down, they were showing her that she was putting herself in harm's way. And her lack of proper attire is indicative of her fear of being exposed as a frail, old lady. It's quite clear that Betsy is NOT frail. She simply needs to learn her limits and allow herself to take it easy. Nothing feeble about that! After helping Betsy with this dream, she informed me that she hired a neighborhood boy to mow her lawn. Good girl!

The following dream is only one of hundreds I received after the Terror Attacks. Loss and searching was the theme in almost all the dreams:

"Searching for My Daughter"

I am in my home looking all over for my daughter (who in real life is grown and out of the house). I look for her down the hall (searching and searching). I must find her and verify she is okay. I go to her old room but she is not there. Anxiety rising, I turn back to the hallway. Suddenly she appears at the other end but looks ghostly. I say to her, "You're alive! You survived!" but feel doubtful because she looks like an apparition.
- Lydia 54, Hagerstown, Maryland

Lydia had this dream on September 14th, 2001, three days after the Terror Attacks. Her psyche was searching for validation that those near and dear to her were okay, physically AND emotionally. At that time, our nation was consumed with the massive search and rescue effort. This dream shows Lydia's empathy for all those who actually were searching for a loved one. Notice the uncertainty at the end of her dream. She is not sure her daughter is really alive, really a survivor, really safe. That doubt and uncertainty truly reflects the global state of mind at the time, as we were all forced to question the permanence of our safety and freedom.

What have you lost in your dreams lately? Was it something you could do without or was it something you desperately needed? Was it something that you could replace with something even better? When you get a "losing-dream" ask yourself what, in your waking life, you might be better off without. Is there something or someone you really should appreciate more? Is there anything that you oughtta just let go of? Nothing lasts forever, but yet, life has a funny way of presenting us with new and wonderful things after a loss.

ഇ൪ജ൱ൽ

While "losing-dreams" are all about the temporary nature of things around us and within us, "finding-dreams" are all about discovering and acknowledging qualities, abilities and behaviors that are unknown to us.

"Finding Crystals"

My wife and I were hiking up a mountain. Along the way we found this glowing cluster of crystals. I picked it up and put it in my pocket. This allowed us to make it to the top. When we reached the top of the mountain there was a festival with rides and balloons and games. I awoke feeling exhilarated!
- Norman 48, Chattanooga, Tennessee

Mountains are a classic symbol for "high" aspirations and goals. Dreaming of trekking up a mountain reflects the act of reaching those goals. Norman's mountain, in reality, was a struggling, new age newspaper he and his wife were publishing. Crystals are a favorite tool of meditation and healing energy for new-agers, so it is very appropriate that Norman's subconscious used crystals to get his attention. His dream was showing him that he has the focus and energy within him to reach his goals, his mountaintop – a successful publication. Good thinkin' putting it in his pocket! In his dream, the cluster of crystals helped him reach the top where he found a festival, which in Dreamology is a cause for celebration for a job well done!

"Finding Fish"

I'm always dreaming of finding fish. Sometimes I look in my aquarium and there are all kinds of new and different fish in there that I've never seen before. Sometimes I'll be looking into a pond and I'll see a beautifully colored fish, then another, then another. And then I'll find frogs, and salamanders and turtles and sometimes even a dolphin, all in this little pond! –
Rebecca 31, St. Cloud, Minnesota

Rebecca's dream is a recurring dream, which means her subconscious is constantly reminding her of something. Rebecca is a writer, and like all writers she is constantly struggling for inspiration. The pond and the aquarium are both small, contained bodies of water. But to her subconscious, they are the creative juices contained within her mind. All those fish and other aquatic critters are her own creative ideas that are floating around in there. It just so happens that she would get this dream every time she had writer's block. Her dreaming mind was constantly reminding her that she is full of great ideas, and in order for her creativity to thrive, just like a pond or an aquarium, she needs to care for and maintain those creative waters.

"Finding Rooms"

I was with my best friend. We were in this beautiful mansion I've never seen before with marble floors and a spiral staircase. As we walked around we kept finding room after room after room. Suddenly, it became very windy and stormy outside. It became so severe that we feared it might become a tornado so we found a small room with no windows in the back of the house to hide in. - Samantha 40, Cheektowaga, New York

Finding new rooms may be the most common occurrence in "finding-dreams." Houses are the dwelling place of the soul. They symbolize our self and our state of mind. To dream of finding new rooms in a house means you are discovering new and unused parts of your personality, perhaps some new talent or attitude. Samantha had begun taking Yoga shortly before she had this dream. She was surprised at how much she enjoyed her classes and even more so, at the peace of mind it brought her. Yoga was helping Samantha to rediscover herself so it is no wonder she dreamed of discovering room after room in a beautiful mansion. The storm in her dream symbolizes the turmoil in her life. She was on the verge of a messy divorce. Her dream was reaffirming what her Yoga classes were teaching her – she has a big, beautiful personality with lots to offer. Yet, there is a safe, small place deep inside of her she can always go when life gets stormy.

"Finding an Old Chandelier in the Basement"

I was in my basement looking for something when I found a crystal chandelier in a drawer of an old dresser. I was excited to discover that it was the chandelier that hung in the foyer of my childhood home. I pulled it out slowly, thinking it would be very heavy, but it was actually very light. That's because it turned out to be missing quite a few crystals. I didn't care. I couldn't wait to show it to my husband so we could decide where to hang it in our house.
- Liz 30, Boston, Massachusetts

In Liz's basement, she finds something a bit more pleasant than what was waiting for poor Bethany. Liz found a crystal chandelier; a relic from her past. Chandeliers are beautiful and elegant reflections of one's Inner Light. Liz's chandelier reflects the light that was ignited during her childhood while in that home – the many faceted values and ideas that were passed on to her by her family. Liz had, unknowingly, stored that Inner Light away for quite some time until she came to a point in her life where she could find a use for it and bring it into her own home. The missing pieces to the chandelier are for Liz to fill in with her own values and belief system. Liz had this dream shortly after she learned she was pregnant with her first child.

"Finding-dreams" aren't always about discovering positive elements to one's life. Sometimes the things we find in a dream will reveal something that needs immediate attention:

"Finding Bones"

I was digging in the ground and found a dead body. I put the body in a box and buried it outside. I didn't tell anyone because I was afraid I would get into trouble. But then someone began to dig where I had buried the body. I stopped them before they found anything. Part of the box was showing and a hand was coming out like the person inside had been trying to get out. I woke up before anyone noticed the hand or the box. There was no more sleep that night. Every time I closed my eyes the box was there.   - Jessie 28, San Antonio, Texas

Digging is a form of searching. Consciously, Jessie did not know she needed closure to an old issue. Yet subconsciously she was searching, "digging" deep into her past to unearth something she thought she had buried long ago. That issue is the abuse she suffered as a child, and what was bringing it back to the surface was the birth of her own child. The guilt she feels in the dreams is similar to the guilt she felt way back then, always afraid she was going to get in trouble, always feeling everything was her fault. This dream helped Jessie to realize that burying all those old memories and the feelings associated with them was not going to make it all go away. Now that she had a child of her own, she decided to seek therapy to help her heal from the trauma of her childhood so that she could ensure a happy one for her little girl.

Are you finding interesting objects in your dreams? What is the nature of your new discovery? Does it excite you or does it repel you? Is it something you need? Is it something you want? Or is it something you wish you hadn't found? Now that it has been found, what would be the proper thing to do with it? No matter what it is that you find, remember that it is a part of you or a part of your life. It has revealed itself to you to because it needs your attention. It needs you to acknowledge it so that you can utilize it or overcome it. The things we discover in our dreams are our own personal treasure trove of information and guidance.

ಬಂಗ3ಬಂ

"There is always light shining in the darkness for those who dare to open their eyes at night."
- Richard Bach

Artist: Nicole Bellenfant   **Medium:** Manipulated photography

Chapter Five

Body Language

ಖುയ್ಯುಆ

"Invisible Arm"

I am in my old bathroom at my parents' house. I am standing in front of the mirror, brushing my hair when I notice that my right arm is invisible. My sister walks in and screams at the sight of the hairbrush moving by itself. I go downstairs and find my mother and show her that my arm is invisible. She tells me that it is not invisible; it is actually in the freezer! "You just need to take it out and let it thaw so you can put it back on in time for school, dear." .

Needless to say, I had to feel around and make sure my arm was really there after I awoke from *this* dream! Strange things often happen to our bodies in dreams. Our bodies are our temples, the dwelling place of the soul and it's important that all aspects of our temple are functioning properly in order to make the most of this life. So when some bizarre affliction occurs in our dreams, it's time to take notice and find out what part of the self is not working in unison with the rest of the self.

In my dream my right arm disappeared! Arms enable us to create, to express ourselves and to do whatever we want or need. So I knew this dream was telling me there was something "missing" in the do-it department. At the time of this dream, my oldest sister and I were doing trade shows together. I was selling my artwork on T-shirts and greeting cards while my sister was selling her handmade jewelry. Every show we did, she sold more than I. The reason was that she was a far better salesperson. She would bring customers into the booth while I just waited idly by for someone to take notice. In my dream, my mother told me that my arm was actually in the freezer. My dream was showing me that I do have the ability to create more sales for myself; I do have the tools I need to "grab hold" of those customers. My mother symbolizes my inner nurturer. So at that time, I needed to nurture the ability within me that had been put in cold storage. It was also a learning process, hence the reference to school.

"Teeth Falling Out"

My teeth were loose and crumbly yet I was grinding them and making the situation worse. One fell out, then another, and then I could feel others that were becoming looser. I remember feeling panicked and thinking, "What can I do now to make the others not fall out?"
  - Amy 31, Knoxville, Tennessee

Losing teeth is the most common dream of bodily affliction. This is because anything having to do with the mouth will symbolize verbal expression and so many of us simply don't watch what we say. In Amy's case, the loose teeth were indicative of the loose speech she had been using with her husband. Notice how she was also grinding her teeth. Teeth grinding is often associated with anger. She had been spewing hurtful and demeaning things at her husband out of anger and not thinking about how it was affecting him. Her dream was reprimanding her by saying, "What you have been saying, young lady, is so rotten your teeth oughtta just fall right out of your mouth!" In her dream she asks what she can do to keep the others from falling out. This was her intuition, her wiser self, coming to the realization that she needed to put a stop to this behavior before things got worse. After this dream, Amy knew she needed to keep those loose teeth and loose words where they belong… in her zipped mouth!

"Gum Stuck in My Mouth"

For the past month or so I've been dreaming that my mouth is stuffed with bubblegum and I can't clear it out. I'll be in different places like a restaurant or work. Usually I end up trying to dislodge it from my teeth but it's stuck all over my gums. What's that all about?
  - Jayne 32, Boston, Massachusetts

Ah, the good ol' "can't get this gum out of my mouth" dream! This type of dream is almost as common as the "teeth falling out" dream, yet the meaning for this one is the exact opposite. Whenever you find yourself plagued by a sticky and hostile wad of terror at night, you can bet there is something you need to say or express during the day. For Jayne, that something was the fact that she was falling in love with a certain young man she had been dating and she was afraid to tell him for fear of running him off. Not coincidentally, she would have this dream almost every night she saw him. These dreams were trying to tell Jayne that she needed to free herself… and her oral cavity. The time had come to just "spit it out!"

"Enormous Tongue"

I walked up to my friends at a party and said, "But what about me?!" No one would respond or even look at me. Each time I spoke it was harder and harder to form the words. By the end of the dream my tongue was so swollen and long that it reached the ground! I've had this same type of dream several times. - Phoebe 27, Spartanburg, South Carolina

This dream is another good example of something gone wrong in the verbal expression department. Phoebe's tongue essentially became inflated. Knowing that any part of the mouth symbolizes the way we communicate, it's quite clear that an inflated tongue points to inflated speech… gossip. Phoebe's dreaming mind stretched her tongue to show her what she looks like when she stretches the truth, and it wasn't terribly attractive. Just as in Amy's dream, Phoebe poses a question to herself, "What about me?" Phoebe's wiser self was asking, "What is it about you that could cause others to not respond to you?" She had this dream more than once, which is a good indication that this is an issue that she needs to *lick* before it gets out of hand!

"Missing Face"

I was preparing to go to work. When I looked at myself in the mirror I had no face!
- Daniel 24, Sedona, Arizona

Again, we have a missing body part, which tells us Daniel is lacking something. The face, in dreams, is often a pun on "facing the facts." Daniel's missing face reflects his inability to face something that was going on around him. His dream had him preparing to go to work, which means the issue is something at work. It turns out that Daniel knew his co-worker had been stealing from the company, and although Daniel liked his co-worker he knew that if he told on him the guy would be fired and possibly prosecuted. Daniel did not want to face the truth, nor his boss. Our dreams mirror our deepest thoughts, hopes and anxieties… and the mirror does not lie!

"Rapidly Growing Hair"

I dreamed that the hair on the left side of my head had begun to grow incredibly fast. All the hair: head hair, whiskers, eyelashes, everything. It grew and grew, growing both long and THICK. When I'd pull out a whisker, it had ROOTS in my skin, like the roots on a scallion.
- Jimmy 29, Memphis, Tennessee

Jimmy's dream shows an overabundance of something. Because hair comes from the head, it symbolizes thoughts and ideas. Jimmy's hair was only growing on the left side, which would indicate left-sided thinking. All that growth is showing Jimmy he's overly analytical. Jimmy informed me that his father is this way too, which explains the roots he pulled out. Clearly, the problem comes from his "roots." This dream was a cry from Jimmy's psyche to find a balance in his mode of thinking.

"Gigantic Breasts"

I was standing in my driveway noticing that my breasts were gigantic! A car pulls up and two men get out and come at me. I happened to have this long spear looking thing so I stabbed one guy through the head with it and then thrust it behind me and killed the other guy.
- Dawn 25, Portland, Oregon

Breasts, in dreamland, serve a deeper purpose than the reflection of one's desire to fill out a sweater! Breasts are the great nurturers, the producers of life-sustaining milk that is designed specifically for each mother's precious, helpless little bundle. Breasts in dreams actually symbolize the ability to nurture and care for someone or something.

In Dawn's case, her "bodacious" desire to nurture came about when a stray dog in her neighborhood was hit by a car. She took it to the emergency veterinarian but they were unable to save it. Since Dawn was unable to nurture that ill-fated dog back to health, she went to her local pound and rescued a dog that was scheduled for "termination" that very day. The two men in her dream symbolize the hostile forces that caused the two dogs to be in harm's way. Dawn eliminated the evil forces by "fighting back" with her caring nature.

"Stomach Surgery"

I was in my bathroom. All my insides were exposed. I was trying to remove my stomach with a Q-tip. I heard my brother calling me from the den so I held all my guts in place and went to find out what he wanted. He wanted to know when I was going to cut his hair. I told him that I was a little busy and I couldn't do it right then. - Nicole, 27 Memphis, Tennessee

The stomach takes in and processes food so that the appropriate nutrients can be distributed throughout our body. To the dreaming mind, the stomach symbolizes our ability to take in and process information, thoughts and ideas. Nicole was trying to remove her stomach, indicating her desire to NOT process certain information. There was something going on that she just couldn't "stomach." And that something was the fact that her brother was cheating on his wife. Notice how Nicole's insides were exposed in her dream. Not only could she not "stomach" the information, she also did not want to "spill her guts" to her sister-in-law. As Nicole tries to deal with this situation her brother asks her to cut his hair, which is symbolic of Nicole's wish that her brother "cut short" his very bad behavior.

"Toes Growing Out of My Calf"

I've been having these strange dreams about my body. In the first one I have five toes growing out of my calf. The doctor tells me he can remove them but they will probably just grow back. In the second dream I am face down on an operating table. A doctor is putting a CD-ROM into my back. My husband, my sister and several other people are in line behind the doctor. They all have their own CDs of instructions they want to insert into the CD-ROM. Despite my protests the operation continues. - Linda 33, Las Vegas, Nevada

Is this anything I should be concerned about, Doc?

Both of Linda's dreams are commenting on the way she stands up for herself, or rather the way she DOESN'T stand up for herself. Legs and feet allow us to stand up and move forward. Those toes growing out of Linda's leg in her dream could very well be the beginnings of a new foot. It's not something she can remove, so it must be something her subconscious feels she needs. A new foot would allow her to "take more steps" in reaching her goal of standing up for herself, plus it would also make her stance stronger. Linda's second dream shows us why she needs that extra foot – she needs to "put her foot down" about the way her family treats her. Linda's husband was also her boss. Unfortunately, his orders didn't stop after five o'clock. Her sister, who lived down the street, had a habit of continually pointing out Linda's faults and her mother relied on Linda to help her with her ailing husband. Linda's second dream was showing her that she didn't have a backbone; she had a receptacle that processed other people's instructions. These dreams were using Linda's body parts as metaphors to show her where her weaknesses lie and where she can find her inner strength.

"My Husband's Legs"

I was shopping in a mall but the weird thing was that I was sitting on my husband's legs! No body, just legs. His legs were walking around taking me to any store I wanted to go to. – Beth 28, Richmond, Virginia

Okay, so Beth's dream is about her husband's body parts rather than her own, which rules out that there is something wrong with her temple. In fact, this dream is commenting on how her husband has been a nice addition to her temple as his legs symbolize his ability to support her. Whether it's financially, emotionally, spiritually, or all of the above, he's someone Beth can lean on – or sit on, which is what she seems to prefer. His support allows her to obtain the material things in life that she desires which is why the dream placed her – and her husband's legs – in a mall.

29

"Detachable Penis"

I had this bizarre dream that before my husband left for work he took off his penis and gave it to me. Well, I didn't know what to do with it so I hid it in my shirt. But it kept poking out! When my husband came back home I asked him if he wanted it back and he said that I should keep it.
  - Lynn 26, Nashville, TN

In dreams, sexual organs are the ultimate metaphor either for masculine energy (assertiveness, determination, and the ability to make decisions), or feminine energy (sensitivity, creativeness and passivity).

In Lynn's dream, while it was very considerate that her husband left his penis behind for her, what he's really doing is urging her to be more assertive in life. Lynn couldn't decide what she wanted to do with her life. She had a habit of quitting projects shortly after taking them on and hated her job, yet she was afraid to face her boss with her concerns. Her husband was always pushing her to stand up for herself and her dreaming mind was re-enforcing this by transferring her husband's "manhood" over to her. But Lynn was uncomfortable with this "tool" and rather than take the opportunity to utilize it, she hid it away. She tried to give the darn thing back to hubby, showing her desire that he be the one to play the assertive role, but he told her to keep. Nicole's dream, again, is urging her to take that masculine energy and "play around with it."

"Worm in My Wrist"

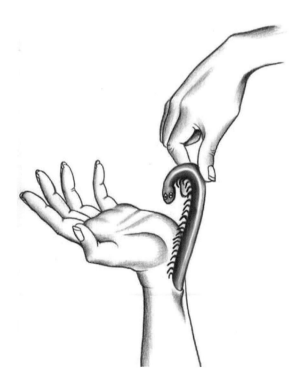

I am living with pain in my left arm. I have seen several doctors and healers and it looks like my pain is nothing but suppressed emotions. A few weeks ago I had a dream that I squeeze my left wrist and out of the hole comes a worm. It's huge and white. I keep pulling it out. It has one hundred legs.
  - Vera 42, Taos, New Mexico

This dream shows us how the body and the mind can work together in solving an issue. The pain in Vera's wrist was letting her know something was wrong. The dream Vera had about her wrist was giving her clues as to the source of the issue. The worm not only reflects that Vera's pain, as well as not knowing the cause of her pain, was really "bugging" her, but worms also feed off of decay, which in dreamology is negativity. Her subconscious was showing her that her pain was feeding off the negative energy that was surrounding her. So Vera was forced to ask herself what or who in her life was causing the negative energy? What or who has "wormed" its way into her peaceful world? It turns out that Vera's boyfriend was part of the problem. The other part of the problem was the way Vera would respond to him. He did not

30

treat her very well and she was afraid to voice her opinions in fear of hurting his feelings. After this dream, Vera realized she needed to remove her boyfriend from her life just as she removed the worm from her wrist.

Our dreams will use all sorts of interesting symbols to relay messages to us. The next time your dream uses parts of your body, be sure to ask yourself what that particular body part helps you to do in waking life. What is happening to it in your dream? How is it making you feel? What could you do to "heal" the situation? What is going on in your waking life that seems similar to what is going on in your dream? Keep in mind that every part of your body is a part of you, your person. So when your dream is about your body you can bet it's commenting on your personal behavior and issues. Listen to your body language, it's not that hard to understand.

ॐ๛ॐ

"Am I a man dreaming that I am a butterfly or a butterfly dreaming that I am a man?"
- Chuang-tzu

Artist: Lauri Quinn Loewenberg   **Medium:** Water color/Color pencil/Digital media

Chapter Six

Talk to the Animals

ഇയ്യള്ളൂറ

"Orca on the Porch"

I am at my parents' house looking out the window at the view of the city (my parents' house is on top of a mountain with a beautiful view of Tennessee). As I gaze at the view, the city morphs into an ocean and rises up the mountain to my parent's porch. An Orca leaps out of the water and I rush out to the porch to get a closer look. As it swims underneath the porch, its dorsal fin sticks up between the slats of wood. I try to touch the fin but I miss; it is going too fast. It comes back out from under the porch and leaps out of the water one last time. I reach out and finally touch it. As it falls back into the water, my hand slides across its slick, wet body. We've made a connection and I feel fulfilled. I go back inside and my entire family is there, my grandmas, aunts, uncles, cousins, everybody. Someone slices a cake I had made and we all eat.

This was one of those dreams where you wake up and exhale a big, "Oh wow!" It was magical. Just as in waking life, animals in our dream life can amaze us. But they can also frighten us, amuse us and comfort us. The emotion our dream animal evokes within us reflects how we feel about something that is going on in the real world. And the qualities that we attribute to that animal also symbolizes a part of our own personality or the way we are behaving at that point in time.

The size of the beast in my dream is indicative of the significance of the dream. In waking life I had just earned my Black Belt in Tae Kwon Do – a *whale* of an accomplishment! I also believe an Orca was my dream animal that night because Orcas are black and white and, with the new addition of my Black Belt, so was my ghee (martial arts uniform). My dreaming mind placed me at my parents' house because it is on the top of a mountain and, as we discussed in chapter four, mountaintops in dreams are often goals – I had reached my martial arts goal! The awe I felt as I touched that enormous creature was not unlike the amazement I had for myself. It sounds trite, I know, but it was a really big deal! If you haven't figured it out by now, I'm a fairly passive and meek individual. But I did it. I stuck to it, worked hard at it and I reached my mountaintop and made contact with the Killer Whale inside of me. So you see, with a little effort, you can have your cake and eat it too!

"Walking the Fish"

I was shopping in a really swanky area, like Beverly Hills. I was dressed in the finest clothes and I looked fabulous but I was walking a fish! It didn't at all seem strange.
 - Natalie 34, Buffalo, New York

Fish are one of my favorite dream symbols because I happen to dream about them… a lot! Fish are something we catch, keep, or eat. Inturn, a fish could symbolize something you want – something you are "fishing" for, something you have contained, or something you need in order to "nourish" your mind or spirit. In Natalie's dream she is taking her fish for a stroll, which shows us that she has already "caught" what she was "fishing" for and is now utilizing it in her daily life. It turns out that Natalie had been attending a church that her friends were pushing her to join. She found great comfort and inspiration from this church. She had "caught" the spirituality for which she had been searching. This dream was not about enriching her closet. It was about enriching her mind and spirit. Natalie's dream was showing her that she wears her spirituality well!

"Giant Frog in my Bed"

Last night I dreamt that I woke up and a giant frog was sitting on my bed. I tried to shoo it away by yelling at it and throwing my book at it but it just sat there. It didn't even flinch! - Patty Ann 34, Richmond, Virginia

Notice how Patty Ann woke up in her dream. This will happen when there is something we need to "wake up" and pay attention to in real life. Patty Ann woke up to a giant frog on her bed. Frogs are most commonly known for leaping. Her dream was warning her about something she was about to "jump" into.

Patty Ann had this dream only days before she was going to move in with her boyfriend of six weeks. She had not even filed for divorce from her estranged husband yet. She was unable to get the frog to move because her dreaming mind was telling her that, just like Kermit, she needed to stay put for the time being.

"German Shepherd Pate"

I was at the end of a driveway with two German Shepherds. I didn't know if they were friendly so I crouched down to their eye level. One came running up to me all happy. The second one was a little unsure so it crawled up to me. I pet the first dog and then I started to eat it!!! The first dog's back legs turned into a pate substance and I was scraping it off with a cracker and eating it. The dog seemed fine with this. I woke up feeling sick that I had eaten dog!
– Sandra 40, Bowen Island, British Columbia

Believe it or not, chowing down on our four legged friends is not an uncommon dream theme! Since dogs most often symbolize loyalty and companionship, and so many of us "hunger" for these things in our lives, we might find ourselves enjoying a nice Fido sandwich from time to time – or in Sandra's case, a German Shepherd pate. The breed of the dog can play an important role as well. German Shepherds, which are known to be guard dogs or police dogs, may appear in our dreams when we feel a little guarded or insecure about something. Sandra was insecure and guarded about a new relationship she was in. She was unsure of her new boyfriend, just as the one dog was unsure of her in the dream. Yet she "hungered" for the security and companionship her new beau could offer. So her dreaming mind turned the German Shepherd – the security dog – into a tasty pate as if to say, "Come on! Dig in! Give it a try. Let this relationship *nourish* your soul. Bon Appetit!"

"Skateboarding Husky"

My Husky was skateboarding in the empty pond in my backyard. I was really impressed. I told her to keep practicing because I wanted to get her on the Stupid Pet Tricks segment on David Letterman. After I told her this she fell off and bumped her nose on the side of the pond.
– Andrew 28, Louisville, Kentucky

The dog in this dream takes on a slightly different meaning since this is the dreamer's own pet. In waking life, most of us will train our dogs to some degree. Whether that means training them to jump through flaming hoops or simply to not piddle on the carpet, we take control of them and teach them to be obedient. So Andrew's pet Husky symbolizes something in his own life he is trying to get under control. At the time of this dream, Andrew was preparing to audition for the lead role in a play at his local community theater. He felt pretty confident that he could "skate" through the audition with flying colors, which was exactly the part of himself he was trying to train – his overconfidence! The breed of dog is important in this dream too. Huskies are sled dogs. Andrew's subconscious mind was associating the task of pulling a heavy load to the heavy burden of perfectionism he was placing on himself. His dream was warning him that, in his effort to receive recognition and fame, he might wind up falling flat on his face.

"Cat on Grandma's Head"

I was walking up the stairs and halfway up I bumped into my grandmother. She had a beautiful tabby cat on top of her head!
- Tammy 32, Greenville, South Carolina

Cats are fun dream animals! They are independent, aloof, sneaky, sexy, and some would say even a bit intuitive. Cats are also associated with feminine qualities, while dogs are associated with masculine qualities. And rightly so, I suppose, since women tend to dream of cats more than men do. For Tammy, her dream cat symbolized her independence. Tammy was moving upward in her career as a real estate agent and she was considering breaking off from the company she worked for and starting her own agency. Her grandmother was widowed at a fairly young age and had to enter the work force to support her children and even continues to work to this day. So Tammy's grandmother has always represented the independent career woman to Tammy's subconscious. The cat was on her grandmother's head because it symbolizes independent "thinking." That mode of thinking was something Tammy learned from her grandmother. And just as it is with dogs, the breed of the cat can often play a role in the meaning of the dream. Her dreaming mind used a Tabby as a play on the name Tammy. The cat and her grandma are both a part of Tammy's independent nature and will help her on her climb up the stairway of success.

"Angry Kittens"

I'm inside a covered bridge, like the one from <u>The Bridges of Madison County</u>. There are several white kittens milling around me. Then I notice one black kitten sitting atop a chair. For some reason I feel sorry for it so I pick it up. It hisses at me and I fear it will harm me so I throw it down. The white kittens begin mewing noisily and I feel that they are talking about me. – Candace 45, Alexandria, Minnesota

Candace's dream shows us how cats can symbolize sexuality. Candace was in a relationship where marriage was a very real possibility. But she'd been married and deeply hurt before and was afraid to let her current relationship move forward. So, in her dream, we see her in a covered bridge. Bridges symbolize transition, crossing over to a new point in one's life. The transition Candace was trying to make was in the romance department so her dream bridge was reminiscent of a very romantic story. The kittens on the bridge are her inner "sex kitten!" The white kittens are milling about her, wanting her attention. They are the parts of her sexuality that want to play. They are white because that is the color of purity and of new beginnings. The black kitten on the chair is the part of her sexuality that is just "sitting around." It's black because that is the color of the unknown, the mysterious. And the unknown is what was holding her back. But notice how she is drawn to the black kitten in the dream. She feels sorry for it. That's because it is a part of herself that she has isolated and ignored. So it has become hostile. Whenever there is a hostile character in our dreams, it's a good indication there is something in our lives that we have ignored. Candace's dreaming mind used irresistible little kitties to draw her attention to something she had been ignoring, her playful sexuality.

"Tiny Lion"

I was at a circus. A man that was wearing long robes and looked like Moses came over to me. He was holding a pet carrier. He opened it up and pulled out a teeny, tiny adult, male lion. He then handed it to me. It fit perfectly in the palm of my hand. It was so cute! I felt like this lion was mine now and I was very excited about it.
- Gwynn 32, Spartanburg, South Carolina

Lions are most often associated with courage and power. They are "the kings of the jungle" so they can symbolize one's leadership abilities. Gwynn's dream lion was very tiny, which means it is an underdeveloped or "dwarfed" part of her personality. When Gwynn had this dream, she had just moved to Spartanburg, wrecked her car on the way and found that her new job did not offer the benefits she was promised. Naturally, she was feeling that her life was a three-ring circus. Her dreaming mind stepped in and offered her some encouragement. The man in the robes is a metaphor for her inner wisdom and he came bearing gifts! His gift to her is a little, tiny bit of courage. It's not much but it's there and it's hers. Gwynn's dream is telling her it's "in her hands" now to muster up that dab of courage and take on the chaos in her life. The more she uses her courage and nurtures that little lion within, the more it will grow. Grrrreat dream, don't you think?

As many dreams as I have worked with over the years, I am continually amazed at how often snakes will slither into our dreamscape! Snakes can mean several things when they appear in our dreams: a healing energy, a fear or temptation, or a masculine energy. The healing aspect of snakes in dreams comes from waaaay back in ancient times when snakes were believed to have healing properties, probably due to their ability to regenerate their skin as well as their powerful venom which they use to protect themselves. This belief has embedded itself into Greek and Roman mythology and over time evolved into the caduceus, the two snakes wrapped around a winged staff, which is a symbol used by today's modern healers – physicians. The temptation aspect of snakes in dreams comes from the ol' Adam and Eve story where Satan disguised himself as a snake to entice Eve into taking a bite out of the forbidden fruit from the Tree of Knowledge. The masculine aspect of snakes is due to their phallic shape and the fear aspect is obvious – they're pretty creepy!

"Snake Soup"

I am in the living room, with my five-year-old son, eating soup for dinner. The soup is made of small black snakes. My son tells me he is still hungry so I go to the kitchen where there is a very large, black snake slithering around. I pick it up and begin to cut its head off with the intention of cooking it. As I am cutting its head off it literally makes me sick and I go in the other room to vomit, then come back to the kitchen to finish cooking the snake. - Abby 26, Moberly, Missouri

Abby's dream involves all of the meanings above. She and her son are eating snake soup because they both "hunger" for some *masculine energy* in their lives (Abby is a single mom). Soup is also supped when one is sick so this shows that bringing a good, strong man into the fold will *heal* their situation. But notice how Abby gets sick when she cuts the head off the big snake. This is because, at the time of her dream, there was a particular man she was *tempted* to bring into their lives but she *feared* might not be good for them in the long run. It had the potential to turn into a "poisonous" situation. Chopping off the head reflects her inner desire to separate that idea from the picture.

"Giant Snake in my Bedroom"

I went into my bedroom and found a giant, evil anaconda on my bed. Of course I ran out terrified and told my mom, but she didn't really listen to me and just pooh-poohed my concerns and made me go back into the bedroom, alone by myself, saying that whatever was bothering me couldn't be that bad. So I went in there and had to go to bed and supposedly fall asleep when all the while there is an evil monster of a snake lurking and crawling all around me.
- Ann 25, Germantown, Tennessee

Ann by nature, was a worrier and at the time of this dream she was having health issues that added to her full plate of worry. The snake in Ann's dream plays two roles, the fear role and the healing role. She was associating her health problems with a poisonous snake lurking in her bed – it's only a matter of time before it strikes and things get worse. The snake was also gigantic, reflecting that she was making a bigger deal out of her situation than it really was. On a deeper level, the snake slithered into her dream to let her know it was time to heal. She needed to heal her mind of worry as well as heal the minor health issues she was suffering. "Get thee to a physician," says her dreaming mind. Her mother is her own wise and nurturing instincts. This part of her mind is telling her that everything is going to be just fine, and that she may indeed be making a mountain out of molehill.

Sometimes the animals in our dreams are unusual creatures of our own making, reflecting our very own unique personality traits:

"Mix-Matched Animals"

I needed a place to live so I moved into this trailer. There was a woman there too, who told me to stay out of her laboratory a.k.a. her half of the trailer. She kept an animal called the "lion pig" in a glass case. It was just a lion that was the size of a pig. She also had a killer whale the size of a gold fish and something called a "rhino-pig." I decided to liberate the animals at a huge outdoor aquarium. The fish at the aquarium began to die off as soon as I released the animals. - Hunter 23, Memphis, Tennessee

Just when you thought you'd heard them all, huh? Ahem. Okay. Hunter is a struggling standup comic. He has all sorts of, uh, shall we say bizarre and eccentric ideas which he would like to put into his routine. The lady in this dream is the part of his personality that is sensitive and wants to keep those creative ideas bottled up. She is the part of Hunter that is overly concerned with what others, especially his family, would think of his jokes. So let's take a look at these animals. Even though they seem completely off the wall, they actually reflect Hunter's situation perfectly. There is a "lion pig," which is a combination of bravery and crudeness. Hunter needs to be brave in order to use his crude jokes on stage. There is a Killer Whale that is the size of a goldfish. This is something big that is being dwarfed by his inhibitions. It is also a pun on what all comedians want their jokes to do – " kill." And finally, we have the "rhino-pig." Rhinos are known for their very thick skin and pigs, as stated earlier, for their crudeness. This animal is telling Hunter he needs to be thick-skinned in order to deal with the criticism he will get from his crude jokes. This dream is telling Hunter that freedom of expression is good… but beware! When expressing wildly creative locked-up talents, be sure it's in an appropriate forum because other ideas, connections, and friendships might "die off" when that bizarre stuff is revealed to the public.

What kinds of animals inhabit your dreams? What qualities do you associate with your dream animal or animals? Do you recognize those qualities in yourself? How is your dream animal behaving? Is it wild and out of control or is it meek and timid? Are you behaving that same way somewhere in your life?

Your dream animals are trying to teach you something about yourself. Talk to your dream animals. What do you think that horse you dreamed about last week would say to you? "Come on. Get back in the saddle! You can do it." Perhaps that eagle from last night was saying, "Look at me. I symbolize freedom. It's time to free your self! It's time to soar!" I think my dream Orca was telling me, "See? I've always been right at your fingertips. All you had to do is believe!"

ಏಓಜ಼ಲಞ

"I've dreamed in my life dreams that have stayed with me ever after and changed my ideas,
they've gone through me like wine through water, and altered the color of my mind."
– Cathy Earnshaw in Emily Bronte's Wuthering Heights

Artist: Lauri Quinn Loewenberg   **Medium:** Water color/Color pencil

Chapter Seven

Water World

ഇൻദ്യൻ

"I Found Myself Face Down in a Pool"

I am swimming in the deep end of an Olympic size, indoor swimming pool. There is a large object at the bottom of the pool, though I can't make out what it is. It slowly rises to the top and when it finally surfaces I see that it is a girl with long red hair. She is floating face down. I push on her to see if she is okay. She rolls over and I see her face. It's me and I'm dead! I climb out of the pool in horror and as I'm running I bump into a toilet. It is full of brown, thick muddy water. I flush the toilet and watch the muddy gunk go down the drain. Suddenly, I feel great!

Water in dreams symbolizes the emotional realm. While water is a common element to everyone's dreams, we of the fairer sex, being the emotional creatures that we are, dream of water an awful lot! Just as the oceans ebb and flow, so do our emotions and so do the fluids of our bodies. Water can be cleansing and refreshing just as it can be overwhelming and threatening. The condition of the water in our dreams will mirror the state of our emotions and for us gals, the state of our cycles.

I had the above dream about a month after my son was born. I suffered greatly from Postpartum Depression. I cried all the time, and as much as I loved and adored my son, I felt guilty for bringing him into the world. I was overwhelmed with awe and love for this precious new life, yet riddled with guilt and despair that this perfect and innocent little child was just going to die someday. Bringing life into this world was more than I could bear, and my poor husband could hardly bear my constant flow of tears. Just like in my dream… I was in deep! But thankfully, my dream was marking the beginning of the end of my depression. My dream was showing me that the girl that was drowning in that emotional pool was dead now. It was time for me to pull myself out of it. The toilet was my symbolic vessel that allowed me to "flush away" all that yucky, mucky depression. When I awoke from that dream, I truly felt relieved. And I did get better after that. The deepest part of my depression was indeed gone, and I could now be the mom I was meant to be.

"Manta Rays in the Swimming Pool"

I was swimming in a pool when I saw these two Manta Rays hovering about a foot above the water. I thought they were so beautiful. They began coming toward me. As they got closer I saw that they had long spikes extending out from their mouths. I jumped out of the pool thinking I would be safe. But since they were never in the water they continued to come after me. I ran around the patio trying to escape but I think they ended up stinging me with their spikes.
- Julia 29, Memphis, Tennessee

Here again we have a pool, which signifies Julia's emotional depths. But like the water in the pool, they are emotions she has contained. Now, how about those Manta Rays? They are beautiful yet dangerous. They represent something in Julia's life that is deceptive. Usually, when anything that has the capability of stinging makes an appearance in our dreams, it symbolizes "stinging remarks" or hurtful and "poisonous" words. This is certainly the case in Julia's dream because, in addition to the stinging nature of a Manta Ray's tail, Julia's Manta Rays had spikes coming out of their mouths. The Manta Rays in this dream symbolize Julia's two older sisters. Both of which are beautiful (one is a model and the other a stewardess) but are constantly putting her down. This is why they were "above" the surface of the water. Their cruel remarks kept Julia "down" in her emotional pool. Notice how we also have the "being chased" element in this dream. Being chased always points to avoidance. Julia was afraid to confront her sisters about the way they continually degraded her. Even though she would tend to run from this issue, jumping out of the water shows that she doesn't let it overwhelm her.

"Sofa on the Ocean"

I was sitting in my living room with my mother. I was fishing off the sofa because the living room was floating on the ocean. I was watching a whaling boat in the distance. There was a lot of action on the boat. The men were jumping in and out of the water and climbing up and down the mast. My mother said to me, "Don't worry. You'll catch something."
- Jeff, 29 Beverly Hills, California

The ocean is the largest body of water there is, vast and seemingly endless. So when we find ourselves on the ocean in our dreams, it may very well be referring to an emotional situation to which we see no end. For Jeff, that seemingly endless, emotional situation was two fold… it involved both love and work. Jeff was studying Homeopathic Medicine. He was unsure of how and where to go about building his career once he graduated, and was spending so much time studying to build that elusive career that he had no time to date. He worried about his future as he watched his friends and members of his family get married and start careers of their own. So one night he finds himself sitting in his living room which happens to be floating on the ocean. This emotional issue was affecting his daily life. He is fishing for what he sees others catching. Just like the fishing boat in his dream, there was a lot of action for those around him, but none for Jeff. His mother made an appearance in his dream to comfort him and to encourage him as all good mummies do. And when Mom pops up in a dream, which she does at least once a week, she symbolizes our nurturing side. Jeff's inner nurturer is telling him to hang in there because there are "plenty of fish in the sea."

"Fist Bursting Out of the Ocean"

I dreamed I was married to a white man and we had a huge house on the ocean. For some reason I was sick and had gone to the doctor. I took a cab home. The driver was a black man who looks a lot like my husband. We got along so well that I forgot about being sick and asked him to come in when we got to the house. We went upstairs to a huge library with a wall-sized window overlooking the water. We laughed and joked around. I looked out the window and saw a wall of water that came rushing straight up out of nowhere. As the water resurfaced, a large fist appeared and then it opened to the sky as black vines slowly force it back under the water.
- Sapphire 25, Midlothian, Virginia

Here again we have the ocean, representing a seemingly endless amount of emotional stuff. Sapphire's emotional issues were the result of her marriage. Or perhaps I should say, the result of people's reactions to her marriage. As you can probably gather from the dream, Sapphire is in an inter-racial marriage. It's a happy marriage, and her husband is very loving, but there are people around her that don't like it, which causes a great deal of stress to Sapphire's emotional balance. Notice how in the dream she was "sick" when married to a white man and forgot about her sickness when in the happy company of the black man who resembled her real life husband. Her dreaming mind was reassuring her that she is psychologically healthy and in the relationship she should be. She gazes out a huge window and sees a wall of water rushing up into the air. Windows, in dreams, are portals to reality. They show us how we truly "view" our world around us. That wall of water is an emotional outburst or anxiety attack that threatens to take her over. It is also an emotional wall she has put up as a barrier between herself and those who ridicule her marriage. The fist that emerges from the wall of water is a message from her dreaming mind to stand up for her rights, to "fight the power" (and is, incidentally, the African-American "black power" gesture). Her fist of defiance is being pulled under the waters of emotion. It's almost as if she is being forced into submission and/or forced to feel a certain way. The vines are "clinging" opinions of relatives and co-workers that are dragging her down. This dream was showing Sapphire that her emotions were getting the best of her and "drowning" that fighting spirit within her.

"River of Clothes"

I was watching a river. I began to notice there were clothes floating in the river. More and more clothes were appearing until the river was no longer made of water but clothes... MY clothes!! All the outfits I wear to the office! - Kerri 28, Greenville, South Carolina

This is a perfect example of the kind of dream we gals of childbearing age need to look out for every twenty-eight days or so… the "flowing-water dream!" That mind-body connection we often hear about truly exists. Our subconscious mind is very aware of what is going on with our bodies, often before we even know. Kerri had the above dream just at the onset of her PMS (a fun topic indeed, but nonetheless, it is important enough that our dreams will comment on it from time to time). Kerri's emotional waters appeared to her as a rushing river because it was reflecting the fluid of her body at that particular point in time. But notice how the river transforms into her work attire. Clothing in dreams symbolizes the attitude or personality we "put on" to show the world. Kerri's dream was warning her that, at certain times of the month, she was wearing her emotions on her sleeve. She was letting her monthly flood of emotions "drown" that smart and savvy attitude she normally displays at work.

"Rising Water"

I was with Monica Lewinsky and my two little boys. We were in this room that was about ten stories high. All the walls were made of glass and there was a staircase that went all the way up. Suddenly a storm began to brew outside and waves began to crash against the glass walls. I noticed that water was seeping in from under the glass. The water began to rise very rapidly. There were all kinds of sea-life coming in. There was even an octopus that tried to grab me! I gave Monica one of my boys, I grabbed the other and we began climbing the stairs for safety. The water kept rising and rising. At that point I woke up.
- Jeanne 33, Knoxville, Tennessee

Here we have a "rising-water dream" indicating a worsening emotional situation. Jeanne was in an unhappy marriage. Her husband was a heavy drinker, paid very little attention to their boys and couldn't keep a job. They were going "deeper and deeper" into debt. Jeanne wanted to be a stay at home mom but it was looking more and more like she was going to have to be the one to go out and earn the money. Plus, she wanted her husband out of the picture. The glass room reflects Jeanne's fragile state of mind while the brewing storm outside is indicative of her pent up emotions in need of a release. Jeanne was feeling very vulnerable, in over her head and like a spectacle to be pitied by others. Her subconscious was associating the way she was feeling to

Monica Lewinsky who, at the time of this dream, was dominating the headlines. Jeanne was in deep so her dream presented her with two options. Either let the dark forces of the situation (the octopus) pull her under, or take control and rise above those emotional depths (the staircase). See how Jeanne's dream gave her encouragement? It presented her with a clever metaphor for her situation, one that she was sure to remember and ponder, and it showed her that there was a way out!

"Pouring Rain"

I was walking outside with three or four people. Suddenly, it began to rain so hard like you couldn't imagine. It was pouring. We found a big tree to stay under. It was incredible how much rain there was. It seemed impossible that it could rain that much.
– Carlotta 54, Castleberry, Florida

"Rain, rain, go away. Come again another day." This is not something we should be singing when caught in a downpour in our dreams. Rain symbolizes tears, the physical manifestation of our emotional turmoil. If your *dreamcast* calls for rain then it's time to pull out the Kleenex ® and turn on the water works! Carlotta had the above dream because she wouldn't allow herself to cry. She was miserable at work, hated her job, and wanted desperately to move to a new town to start over but couldn't afford to do so. She kept her feelings all to herself, wouldn't cry about it, and went around in a constant state of anger. Her dream was urging her to cry, to let it all out. Crying, just like rain, has a remarkable cleansing affect. After a good hard rain, all the dirt and debris is washed off the sidewalks and out of the streets. The air smells fresh and all the vegetation perks right up. After a good hard cry you just feel better. You're not quite so angry or sad anymore. All your muscles relax and you feel relieved. Tears, like rain, wash away the negativity. It's a very healthy release.

"Under Water Airplane"

I was on an airplane when water suddenly began to trickle on my head. The plane was not full so I got up and sat in another seat. Again, water began to trickle on my head. The roof seemed to spring a leak right above me no matter where I went in the airplane. I looked out the window and saw that we were traveling underwater.
– Tonya 32, Greenville, South Carolina

45

Any vehicle, in a dream, will show us how we are "traveling" through life. What is interesting about Tonya's dream is that we have a vehicle, which travels through air, traveling through water instead. Right away that indicates that something in Tonya's life is mixed up. Tonya was very happily married, had many friends and had just received a promotion at the law firm where she worked. Essentially, all aspects of her life were "taking off" as indicated by the airplane. You would think her spirits would be "soaring," wouldn't you? Unfortunately, Tonya was very depressed. The recent death of her cousin, who was more like a brother to her, was bringing her down deep into her emotional waters. She was having a hard time moving on and her sadness was beginning to "trickle" into every area of her life. To be completely submerged in water, like the plane in Tonya's dream, is usually a red flag that our emotions are "engulfing" us. But every dream that holds a warning also holds an answer. Tonya's dream was telling her that, like a plane, she IS equipped with the tools that can bring her out of that funk. Just as a plane's seat can be used as a floatation device, so can the memories of her cousin help keep Tonya afloat on her emotional waters.

"Car Being Soaked"

Every now and then I'll dream that I get in my car to go to school and the interior is completely soaked in water. I know I have to get to school so I drive all the way there in a wet car. - Michael 21, Richmond, Virginia

Again we have a vehicle, a sopping wet vehicle but a vehicle nonetheless. Michael's dream is all about how he, like so many other young men out there, travels through life. The water in this dream is different from the water in all the other dreams we have explored so far. Michaels water is not seen and rather than being a threat, it is merely an annoyance… an annoyance he has to live with for the time being. This annoyance I'm speaking of is the emotional uprising (ahem) caused by hormones! Yes, it is a burden carried by young men (and to a lesser degree, young women) across the globe, that hormonal surge that "drenches" the body, often to a point of unruly and naughty behavior. This dream was urging Michael to not allow this kind of thing to get in the way of his priorities. Make the best of it and proceed toward life's ongoing lessons - "school." Ah, the dream of a maturing mind!

"Clear Water"

I'm with my daughter and we are driving home from somewhere. I realize I have made a wrong turn but keep going because I am curious as to what lies ahead. Suddenly my car plunges into the water and is sinking. I manage to get my daughter out before the car sinks and we swim over to an outcropping of rocks in the middle of the water. Neither of us is frightened or feels in danger. I quickly swim back to my car to retrieve the phone. I look down into the water and notice that it is crystal clear with a sandy, pebbled bottom. The water is so clear that I can fully see the car sitting on the bottom, not very deep, maybe 15 or 20 feet down. The water is very comfortable. As I swim back to the rocks, after getting the phone, I realize the water feels so good, warm and clean. I feel so refreshed and happy swimming in it. When I get to the rocks, I find my daughter in the water happily swimming, playing around. I am happy that she is enjoying herself so much. – Candace 45, Alexandria, Minnesota

Remember Candace?   She's the gal from chapter six who dreamed of the kittens on the bridge. Remember how that dream showed us that she was holding herself back from a promising relationship for fear of getting hurt? Well, this latest dream shows us that she finally "made the plunge." Yep, even though she feared it was the "wrong direction" for her life to take, she made that commitment. And notice how the water in this dream is warm, clear and refreshing. That symbolizes Candace's clear thinking, warm emotions and refreshed attitude. In the dream she didn't have much concern for the car. In other words, she's fine leaving behind her old way of traveling through life, fearful and withdrawn. But she does manage to save her phone. A good sign! She wants to keep those lines of communication open, which is the key to a healthy relationship. This dream reflects Candace's new, playful, emotionally balanced self.

When water flows into our dreams it's time to take a look at our emotional balance. The condition of the water will compare with how we are feeling about something in our life such as a relationship, our career, or even our self.   So how is the water in your dreams? Does it make you wanna dive right in or is it threatening to pull you under? Is there a large body of water in your dream or just a trickle? Where is the water in your dream? Is it in a pool, a river, an ocean or is it out of place like in your car or filling up a room in your house? If your water is in an odd place, it may be an indication that you are dealing with your emotions improperly.

Water is the source of all life just as emotions are the source of all decisions. We need clean, healthy water to live just as we need clear and healthy emotions in order to function on a normal, healthy level. Pay attention to what your dream water is telling you. It's there to help keep you afloat in this life.

ഇരുജ്ഞ

"The dream is a little hidden door in the innermost and most secret recesses of the psyche..."
- Carl G. Jung

Artist: Michael Quinn   **Medium:** Color pencil/Digital media

Chapter Eight

Home Improvement

ഌᎧᏜᏜᏬᏣᏡ

"Old Run Down House"

My husband and I are back at our first house, a 1920's bungalow that we rescued and completely renovated. As we are walking through the house we discover that every single room is trashed. None of the renovations we've done are there anymore. It is in worse shape than when we first bought it. Paint is peeling off of every inch of the exterior of the house. The rock group No Doubt is living there. I confront Gwen Stefani, the lead singer, about the condition of the house. I am so upset that I begin screaming at her. "How could you let this happen?! This house was a showplace and look what you've done to it!!" I was screaming so loud that I actually woke myself up.

Houses in dreams are the dwelling place of the soul. They symbolize our self, our state of mind. The type of house, the condition of the house and even the rooms in the house comment on what is going on within our psyche. At the time of my "house dream," I was experiencing daily headaches, many of which turned into migraines. I've always been a headache sufferer but that particular week they were coming fast and furious... and non-stop. I was becoming depressed from the constant pain and all aspects of my life seemed to be falling apart. My subconscious was comparing my deteriorating state of mind to my old house. Like the old house, I was normally all painted up and decorated and ready to show my dolled up self to the world. But the pain was forcing me to stay in bed. So I had to let my hair, my makeup, my column and my home life responsibilities go.

Like most dreams, this one had a positive message for me. At the time of this dream, No Doubt's song "Underneath it All" was in the top 10 and getting constant radio play. So my dreaming mind placed No Doubt in my old home so that I would associate them with their current hit, which goes like this, "You're really lovely underneath it all." Yes, despite my tangled hair, unpainted face and constant, painfully furrowed brow, I guess I was still okay underneath it all.

"Finding New Rooms"

I have had this dream for several years. I am always on the outside of a small house with two or three bedrooms. When I get inside I go from room to room and find that the rooms are endless. The more I walk through the house, the more rooms I see. The rooms are dusty and need decorating. - Jackie 40, Memphis, Tennessee

This is probably the most common type of house dream there is. And it's always a good sign when you get this dream! To find new rooms is like discovering new parts of your self, new abilities and talents you never knew were there, residing inside you! In Jackie's dream she is discovering room after room but the rooms are dusty and need decorating. The difference here is that the rooms are neglected and need updating so these are abilities and qualities Jackie has neglected. She forgot they were there so her dreaming mind keeps giving her this dream as a continual reminder to grab her feather duster, slap on a new coat of paint and open up those doors! It's time to show the world there's more to Jackie than meets the eye.

"Childhood Home"

I have so many dreams that take place at my parent's house where I grew up. Last night I dreamed I was in their living room. I was watching a triangle shaped UFO that was no bigger than a dinner plate land in my parents' back yard. It tried to abduct the porch swing but failed because the UFO was too small. - Denise 29, Buffalo, New York

We'll dream of being back in our childhood home throughout our entire lives. There are many reasons for this. We may find ourselves back within those protective walls when things in our waking life are getting kinda tough and we are in need of that secure, "everything will be alright" feeling. If childhood wasn't so dandy we may visit our childhood home when we're feeling tormented or in trouble. Sometimes our dreaming mind will place us there because we need to examine the way we are raising our own children. And sometimes our dreams take place there simply because we are being childish in waking life and our subconscious is trying to tell us we need to grow up already! It all depends on our memories and how we felt while living there.

Denise visited her childhood home in the above dream because she was having difficulty deciding what religion to raise her child. She was Catholic and her husband was Hindu. She appreciated the way her parents brought her up but was very interested in raising her son as a Hindu, yet her husband was willing to convert to Catholicism. Like the porch swing, Denise and her husband were "swinging" back and forth on the issue. Denise's parents were insisting she raise the boy Catholic. They were still taking on a parental role in her life and treating her like a child, which is why so many of her dreams take place in her parents' home. The UFO is an interesting twist. UFOs have long been symbols for the higher self. If they truly exist, then they are vehicles for a higher, wiser life form. This dream was letting Denise know she needs to "contact" that inner wisdom and nurture it and allow it to grow strong for it will be the ship that will take away all that indecision. As long as she remains indecisive and allows her parents to treat her like a child, she'll continue to have dreams of being back at their home and her higher self, her inner UFO, will continue to be too weak to intervene.

"House Under Construction"

I dreamed my husband and I were living in this very large house that was under construction. All the floors had been installed but there were no walls yet. My husband and I were on the top floor, which was probably about ten stories up. We were noticing that the floor had a slant to it and all of a sudden my husband slid down the slant and fell off. I woke up screaming!
- Barbara 42, Fairhaven, Massachusetts

To dream of a house that is under construction is actually a good sign. It means you are a work in progress, continually striving to make improvements. Barbara's dream is about the life and the state of mind that she and her husband are "building together." The reason her house has so many stories is because she and her husband are always attending workshops and seminars that teach them how to communicate with one another. They continue to aspire to "higher levels" of awareness with each other. But unfortunately, hubby slid right out of the dream! Barbara's dream was letting her know that her husband was losing interest in the never-ending pursuit of enlightenment. While taking action to improve a relationship is certainly a healthy thing to do, too much of a good thing can turn sour. In waking life, Barbara would dismiss her husband's objections to attending so many seminars, but her subconscious wasn't. It was paying attention to hubby's needs and showed Barbara metaphorically what was happening. What Barbara was trying to build was as unreasonable as a ten-story house and was actually posing a threat to the marriage.

"Old Empty House"

I am standing in a doorway of a very large old house. The room I am facing is huge with a fireplace to my right. The room is empty as far as furniture. It seems like I am leaving this house. My grandpa, who died Jan. 1977, is there. He asked me if I wanted to see a picture of my little sister. I told him that I am the youngest. He said, "Joyce (my real sister) has pictures of your little sister. Do you want to see them?" I said, "Grandpa, I'm the youngest in the family." He said, "Joyce has pictures of your baby sister; don't you want to see them?" I laughed and said, "Grandpa, I'm the baby!" - Jeanne 49, Foristell, Missouri

An old house often reflects an old-fashioned or out-of-date state of mind but it can also indicate how you are feeling… old, worn out and in need of repair. And that is precisely what Jeanne's old house symbolizes. One of her sisters had recently died of cancer and her other sister had just been diagnosed with it. With the onset of cancer in her family, Jeanne, though only 49, was feeling that she must be getting old. The lack of furniture in this dream shows that her feeling is actually baseless and "empty." Cancer does NOT mean you are old. She was at the point where she could either "furnish" her mind with these thoughts or she could leave that state of mind behind. As you can see from her dream, she was leaving it behind. Jeanne's grandfather is someone who has died, so he represents something that needs to be "buried" - her feeling of getting old. Notice how she cries out, "I'm the baby" at the mention that there are pictures of a younger sister. Pictures are a way to freeze time. Jeanne was wanting to freeze her youth and hang on to the fact that she is the "baby" of the family. I'm the baby of my family too, so I understand how that is. A little brother or sister coming into the fold would take that part of our identity away. There's something special about being the baby. Even when we're old and decrepit and toothless, we still can say, "I'm the baby!" So this dream was all about Jeanne's desire to stay young at heart and young in spirit. After all, we're only as young as we feel.

"The Winchester Mystery House"

I was being chased through the Winchester Mystery House in San Jose, California by a shadow. I couldn't see it's face, but I could always hear it breathing right behind me. Every time I opened a door or climbed a set of stairs to escape, the way was blocked off or unusable. I'd open a door and there would be a brick wall or a straight drop to the ground, just like in the real house. - Emily 24, Gilbert, Arizona

The Winchester Mystery House was built by the Winchester Rifle heiress, Sarah Winchester, after the death of her husband and daughter in an attempt to appease the many spirits of those killed by Winchester Rifles. With windows in the floors and stairs leading to the ceiling, Sarah hoped the house would confuse the spirits that wished to do her harm. Touring the house is almost like stepping into a dream. It's no wonder one's dreaming mind might use this perplexing architecture to reflect the "framework" of one's state of mind when dealing with a confusing situation.

Emily was very confused at the time she had her dream. She had been lying to her parents about where she was and whom she was with. Her mischievous behavior led to a pregnancy that caused her to feel trapped, alone and even more confused than she already was. Just like in her dream, there was no escape. There is also the element of being chased in this dream, which we now know to mean that Emily is trying to run from something in her waking her life. Shadows, in particular, are symbolic of things we try to suppress pointlessly because our shadows always follow us. Emily's dream was letting her know that the only way out of this chaos was to face and accept her situation and turn it into a positive force in her life. After all, she is the one who built those brick walls and doorways that lead nowhere and so she is the one who can tear them down and start over.

"Wizard in the Attic"

Whaz Uuup?!

I went up to my attic (my house doesn't really have one). When I opened the door there was a wizard in there kicking back on a recliner and drinking a beer! He seemed awfully happy to see me. - Kevin 29, Cheektowaga, New York

Even if your house doesn't have an attic, you do! The attic symbolizes your higher, spiritual self; the place where you store your spiritual thoughts and ideas. What you find in that attic is a good indication of what is going on with your spiritual growth and development. Kevin's got a wizard in his attic – we should all be so lucky! Wizards symbolize enormous potential, an almost magical ability to create what one wants out of life. However, Kevin's wizard is kinda lazy. That's because Kevin had been neglecting his spiritual side. For quite some time he was pursuing a career as a Methodist Minister. But he began to question whether this was what he really wanted to do with his life, so he decided to take a six-month break. During that six months Kevin got lazy, began drinking daily and never made it back to school. Kevin's dream was showing him what was going on up there in his spiritual storehouse. A huge amount of potential was going to waste… and getting fat and bloated! Kevin's wizard was very happy to see him, showing that this higher, spiritual aspect of himself is ready to get it's tuchus out of that La-Z-Boy® and back to waving its magic wand.

"Cars in the Back Yard"

A couple of nights before my wife and I moved in to our new house I dreamed I was in the backyard. As I was standing there, the backyard sort of fell away. I peered off the edge to see where it went only to find a pit full of beat up and rusty old cars and trucks.
– Lou 35, Clarksville, Tennessee

The backyard symbolizes the part of our self that is hidden from view, the part we want to keep private. Lou had been a pretty avid gambler and had even stolen money from his brother and his wife in order to "hit the tables." After his wife left him for a brief period, Lou took control of his weakness and decided to move to a town that was not quite so conducive to gambling. So Lou's new home is not only a new way of life to his conscious, waking mind but also a new way of thinking to his subconscious mind. In Lou's dream, the backyard of his new home falls away to reveal, basically, a junkyard. His dream is warning him that all his old junk, his old behaviors and ways of doing things aren't going to disappear with a physical move. He'll have to make that emotional and intellectual move as well. You can take the guy out of the casino but you can't take the casino out of the guy!

"A Grim Discovery in the Basement"

Basements, like the subconscious mind, exist below the surface. So when our dream takes us into a basement (or anything subterranean for that matter), it is essentially taking us deep down into our psyches, beneath our conscious thinking to a place where we store things we have forgotten, things we want to forget and things we are afraid to know. It's a good thing to go down into our basements and clean out the cobwebs and the clutter every now and then; the same is true for our psychological basements.

I keep dreaming that I go down into my basement and find an old refrigerator. I open it up to see if it might still be working and to my shock and horror, there is a dead little girl inside.
– Bethany 51, Pomona, California

This is a dream that Bethany had been having her entire adult life. Her subconscious was continually calling out to her, urging her to venture inward and downward into her psyche because there was something within her that needed her attention. That dead little girl symbolizes Bethany's childhood. Bethany felt her childhood was "killed off" by the cold and unemotional nature of her parents. Once Bethany became an adult she pushed her childhood, or lack thereof, down into her psychological basement. Assuming it was out of the picture, she went on with her life. But her life consisted of two divorces, no close friends and two unruly children.

Bethany was not very nurturing and had virtually no patience. Whether this is learned behavior or inherited behavior, it was the result of her childhood and the root to her adult problems. Going down into her basement in her dreams was Bethany's inner desire to delve into the past and revive that little girl lost, nurture her back to health and allow her to frolic within her psyche. After Bethany learned what these dreams were trying to tell her, she began therapy to help her learn to accept her past and get back in touch with all those emotions that had been put into "cold storage."

"Gladiolas in the Bathroom"

I've been having a lot of dreams that take place in my bathroom. Usually the bathroom is filthy, the sink is clogged and there are bugs coming out of the toilet!! But most recently I dreamed that I was planting Gladiolas in the floor of my bathroom!
- Marcy 41, Greenville, South Carolina

Bathrooms are where we cleanse, freshen up and relieve ourselves. So when we need to "wash away" negativity or get rid of something we no longer need, we just may find ourselves in the loo in our dreams.

Marcy had been holding a grudge against her younger sister for over a year. She had loaned her sister a nice chunk of change to help her buy a car but her sister never offered to pay her back. Marcy watched as little sis would go on shopping sprees and eat out almost every night and not once mention her debt. But Marcy never mentioned it either so her frustration and tension continued to build. She kept dreaming of her filthy, insect infested bathroom because there was a lot of negativity Marcy needed to "cleanse" herself of. Her sister's behavior was really "bugging" her. She had allowed the frustration to build to the point that it was clogging her ability to "relieve herself" of it and "flush it away." One day her sister asked Marcy why she had been so cold lately. This question unclogged Marcy's emotional drain and she let it all out. The sisters made up, Marcy got her money back and a fertile ground was laid that allowed a new friendship to "flourish." The Gladiolas Marcy planted in her dream not only symbolize a "blossoming" relationship with her sister, they also symbolize Marcy's feelings… she was awfully "glad" to have her little sis back.

"Blowing Up My Friend's Kitchen"

I had this dream that I blew up my best friend's kitchen. I have no idea why I did it. The next morning I was sitting in their breakfast nook when she and her husband came down for breakfast. The whole kitchen was a smoking black hole except for the refrigerator and the kitchen table. I was feeling very guilty as I sat there waiting for them to notice but they went about their morning as if nothing was different. What in the world is this about?
- Kelly 26, Duluth, Minnesota

The kitchen is a place where we prepare food, which we then eat in order to satisfy our hunger and nourish our bodies. So in waking life, whenever you need or "hunger" for emotional, intellectual or spiritual "nourishment," you are likely to have a dream that takes place in a kitchen.

Your dreams may also place you in a kitchen whenever you are preparing, planning or scheming in waking life, you know, when you've got something "cooking" up in the ol' noggin.

In Kelly's dream she blew up her best friend's kitchen. Kelly's friend was very emotionally needy. She was always complaining about her weight, about her nagging mother, about how she never felt good and so on. She "hungered" for Kelly's support and positive attitude but it was beginning to bring Kelly down. Kelly wanted a way out so her dreaming mind compensated her by blowing up her friend's kitchen, a symbol of her friend's need for emotional nourishment. But the dream also shows Kelly's friend going about as though the kitchen were still there and not a smoking, black pit... a very good indication that there's not really anything Kelly could do that would change her friend's ways. Allowing her friend's neediness to destroy their friendship would leave Kelly feeling terribly guilty.

"Alien in the Oven"

I was in my kitchen preparing a pot roast for dinner. When I tried to open the oven to put the roast inside, the door would not open. It seemed something was inside holding the door shut. I peered in the little window and to my surprise there was a little alien in there shaking its fist at me!
- Debbie 31, Richmond, Virginia

Debbie's kitchen dream is commenting on something she was preparing and planning for. The fact that she was *preparing* a pot roast is a pretty good clue. In waking life, Debbie was preparing to invest money in a marketing plan a friend of hers had for an invention. Debbie was beginning to get cold feet because she didn't completely understand the plan; it was "alien" to her. The little green dude in the Kenmore® is a hostile character and remember, hostile characters in dreams represent something we feel threatened by in waking life, something we're avoiding. Debbie had been avoiding telling her friend that she wanted out. The message in Kelly's dream is that, like the oven door, she needs to muster up the strength to "open up" to her friend. Otherwise, she's got a "recipe" for disaster!

What are the houses like that dwell in your dreams? Describe the house in your dream down to every last detail. Do the details remind you of YOU in any way... of your thoughts or of your body? Do your dreams tend to take place in one room more often than in other rooms? What is the room you dreamed about used for in waking life? What aspect of your life or of your self could you improve upon within that room? The house and all parts of the house are important symbols. And like our actual, physical house, it's important that we do a bit of mental home improvement from time to time. Clear out the clutter in your basement, make sure the plumbing in your bathroom allows for the release of heavy flows of negativity and be sure to check your closets for any skeletons! Your home is where your soul and your thoughts reside. Make sure your home is as sweet as your home can possibly be.

ജ‌ഗ്ഗ‌ഇ

"Every night I hope and pray, A dream lover will come my way" - Bobby Darin, "Dream Lover"

Artist: Lauri Quinn Lowenberg   **Medium:** Oil/Digital media

Chapter Nine

Love and Marriage... Sex and Adultery!

"The Reluctant Bride"

I am standing in the bathroom at my grandmother's house. I am wearing a long, beautiful wedding gown. My two sisters are carefully placing flowers in my hair while advising me of the best way to walk down the aisle without tripping over my hem. You'd think I'd be tickled pink at this moment but I'm not. I'm sickened, distressed, and going through every possible scenario in my head that could get me out of this wedding... for I am about to marry my brother! It feels very, very wrong and I want out. The doorbell rings and shortly thereafter, my mother hollers from down the hall that we may begin because Elizabeth Taylor has just arrived."

Dating, marriage and sex are all forms of unions. Dating is when two people come together for a trial run to see if they can work together on a long-term basis. Marriage is when two people come together and commit themselves to each other forever, and sex is the ultimate union where two people come together and actually become one. When your dreaming mind places you in any of these scenarios it is urging you to unite with or take on the qualities or opinions of your dream suitor.

When I awoke from this dream I wanted to jump into a scalding hot shower with a bottle of Clorox®! But as the day wore on and I replayed the dream to myself over and over, I began to get the message. I needed to "unite" some aspect of my brother's personality into my life somehow.

At the time of my dream, the column was beginning to take off and I was doing a lot of radio appearances to promote the column and the website. But the website left something to be desired. With all the traffic I was driving to the site, it really needed to be easier to navigate and more interactive. My husband had taken the site as far as he could, and it was time to find someone who could take it to the next level. First we hired a company that just didn't give us the attention we needed. Next we hired a private individual who did not represent himself correctly. After that, we weren't sure what to do and that's when I had the dream. My dreaming mind does not see my brother as someone for whom it is illegal and immoral to marry. My dreaming mind sees my brother as a computer genius, someone who knows everything and anything having to do with computers. Above all, it sees my brother as someone who can be trusted. My dreaming mind was telling me I needed to "unite" with someone who had those very qualities. And since it was a marriage dream and not a sex or dating dream, it meant I needed to also find someone who would be "committed" to the project at hand. Elizabeth Taylor made an appearance as a reminder that we needed to make sure this union actually worked out this time! We did find that person. He was an old friend of my husband's brother. Maybe that's another reason I dreamed of marrying my brother – brother seems to be the key word here!

"Date with a Stick Man"

I was at this bar (I never go to bars) and my mother was the bartender. She made a comment to me about my date. I turned to look at my date and he was a stick figure! Even though I am married, I was madly in love with him!!
- Olivia 33, Richmond, Virginia

Whether we're happily married or on the prowl, we all get dating dreams. That's because our subconscious wants us to "court the idea" of taking on some quality or opinion that our dream date possesses. Olivia's dream date was, of all things, a stick man! A flaxen haired Romeo he was not. But an important symbol he was! A stick man is very basic and simple. It is one of the first things we ever learn to draw. Olivia's dream is urging her to try and simplify her life. At the time, she was very stressed at her job as a retail clerk. Her boss would schedule her to work certain hours that made it difficult for her to get her child to daycare on time and get herself to night classes on time. But she would bend over backwards and jump through hoops to please her boss. This only made her life more complicated. Olivia needed to ask him if he could "simply" work out a different schedule for her. That's all she really needed to do; it was that "simple." But, in order to do that she needed to let go of her inhibitions, which is why her dream took place in a bar. For most of us, our moms symbolize the part of our self that knows what's best, so Olivia's dreaming mind had her mom doling out the beverages. Olivia's dream was telling her to relax, let go of her inhibitions and just do what she's gotta do. There's no need to let things get complicated. It's really just *black and white*.

"The Mystery Date"

I was out on a date with a guy I could not see. Now I could see his clothes, I just couldn't see him! I vividly remember being in a club with him and dancing and really enjoying myself. It didn't seem unusual to me or anyone else that I was dancing with ... clothes!
– Kathryn 38, Greenville, South Carolina

Ah, the ever-elusive mystery date, forever making an appearance in our dreamscape. Sometimes his or her face is blacked out: sometimes he or she is just felt as a presence and sometimes, as in

Kathryn's case, he's invisible. No matter how he or she shows up, this dark stranger is always a representation of our "unknown" selves. He or she is a part of our personality with which we are unfamiliar, hence the obscurity of his or her character. The male mystery date symbolizes a woman's masculine qualities - assertiveness and the ability to make decisions. The female mystery date symbolizes a man's feminine qualities – sensitivity, creativity and the ability to nurture. When we get these dreams, it means we need to unite with or integrate those opposite sex qualities into our life.

Kathryn had her "mystery date" dream shortly after joining the PTA (Parent Teacher's Association). She was unhappy with the curriculum her daughter's school was using and decided to get involved. After joining, she found that other parents felt the same as she did. They banded together, made a big stink and, eventually, were able to make significant changes in the school. Kathryn discovered that she did have an assertive, take action side and was working in "harmony" with it, which is why her mystery date took her dancing. Her dream was encouraging her to keep up the fancy footwork!

"The Mystery Groom"

I dreamed it was my wedding day. The preacher says, "You may now kiss the groom." So I start to kiss him but he has a paper bag over his head. I have other dreams about being married to the same guy but something is always blocking his face. I want to know who this guy is, or do I already know?
- Andrea 22, Lockport, New York

We gals daydream about our wedding day beginning at a very early age. We dream of the beautiful gown we will wear, the music that will fill the air and the flowers that will adorn the church. Every last detail is dreamed up. So when we have an actual nighttime dream of our wedding, no matter how bizarre or disastrous, we naturally think it is a glimpse into our future. This is not the case, however. Unless you are actually in the midst of planning your own wedding, wedding dreams are all about making a "commitment" to yourself and/or "uniting" with a new quality, behavior or way of thinking.

Andrea was known to all of her friends as a very sweet and generous girl. She was the type of person that would avoid confrontations at all costs. She wanted to make sure everyone around her was happy even if it meant she had to sacrifice. This behavior often led the people around Andrea to mistake her for a doormat. And a doormat is not a good way to go through life… especially when one is fresh out of college as Andrea was. Notice how Andrea's dreams are always of marriage whereas Kathryn's dream is only of a date. That is because Kathryn needed to merge with her masculine self for one particular issue while Andrea needed to make a life-long "commitment" with her assertive, masculine self – 'til death do they part!

"The Mystery Bride"

I am in India, alone on a small gondola floating along the Ganges. A young boy tells me that the priest is waiting so I follow him. We pull up to the pier. As we approach, I see a wedding. The bride is wearing a green and gold dress. The priest smiles and nods at me. I realize that I am the groom. I am elated! I look into my bride's face and she is so beautiful. The priest says the ceremonial vows and we are married. It is very meaningful and very loving.
  - Gavin 34, Warner Robins, Georgia

Gavin had his "mystery bride" dream after recovering from a bout of alcohol and drug addiction. His wedding symbolizes his "commitment" to a life of higher principles and spirituality. The dream takes place on the Ganges River because of its healing and holy properties. Notice how Gavin is able to see his bride's face. This is because he made the commitment before the dream; he was already seeing the results of his waking commitment.

"Marrying my Stepfather"

I was standing in a church in a wedding gown apparently about to get married... to my stepfather! When the preacher asked me if I take him to be my husband I said, "Eeeewww Yuck!! I can't do this!" I ran out of the church and up a tree. A friend of mine found me and tried to talk me into marrying him. I gave her the rings to give back to him.
  - Mallory 27, Cincinnati, Ohio

In Mallory's wedding dream there's no obscure, mysterious groom waiting for her at the end of the aisle. Her groom is her stepfather! So her stepfather symbolizes something that Mallory was trying to "commit" to at that time. Mallory's stepfather had once studied to be a minister but never pursued it as a career. He often spoke with Mallory about his Christian beliefs and philosophies. To Mallory's subconscious mind, he epitomized Christian thought.

At the time of her dream, Mallory was delving into Christian studies and was considering becoming a "Born Again Christian." Her subconscious mind equates her devotion to Christianity as a devotion to her stepfather. But, just as in my wedding dream, Mallory wanted out of the situation. That is the deeply imbedded awareness of the immorality of such a union penetrating into the dreaming mind. However, in Mallory's dream she actually goes so far as to run out of the church and give the rings back. That symbolizes backing out of the commitment. In waking life, Mallory did eventually back out of such a devout way of life.

"Sex with a Stranger"

I was moving out of my old house. Suddenly, I was skateboarding through a busy urban setting landing very intricate tricks, flying off jumps, and doing grinds just like a pro. It felt like there were definitely other people around watching, too. Then I was having sex with an Asian woman that I did not recognize.   – Brett 22, Scarborough, Maine

The "mystery lover" makes an appearance in our dreams as often as the mystery date. The difference however, is that the mystery date is merely urging us to consider a union of qualities whereas the mystery lover indicates that we have already done so. Brett's "mystery lover" dream symbolizes a merger with his creative side. Brett had this dream shortly after graduating from college and starting a new job as a talent rep for a radio-booking agency. Shortly after beginning his job he was promoted to promotional writer for his department, bringing him closer to his true passion, which is creatively working with the written word.

Brett's dream begins as he is moving out of his old house, which shows us that he is "moving out" of an old state of mind into a new one – the mind of a student to the mind of a career oriented professional. Notice how his dream suddenly switches scenes. Our dreams will do this in order to show us how one thing can lead to another, or how one thing HAS lead to another. Brett's psychological move allowed him to "skate" through his new career just "like a pro." His dream switches yet again to a hot and steamy love scene with an Asian beauty. Brett's "excellent performance" at work allowed him to "unite" with his creative side. Brett's creative self is symbolized by an Asian woman because creativity is considered a feminine energy and Brett has a bit of a passion for the gals of the Asian persuasion just as he has a passion for his creativity.

"Sex with a Same Sex Partner"

I was on my back porch with this beautiful, tall black woman. I don't know who she is but in my dream we seemed to be the best of friends. We were having a drink and laughing and the next thing I know she's kissing me and I'm enjoying it. One thing leads to another and well… I woke up very concerned about my sexuality even though I am deeply attracted to my husband.
 – Nina 35, Dallas, Texas

As much as we don't want to admit it, most of us get this sort of dream, and yes, it does leave most of us wondering about ourselves. Fear not children! As you know by now, sex in dreams does not necessarily mean sex nor is it necessarily commenting on your sexual conduct. Remember, to the dreaming mind, the act of sex is two individuals becoming one, two mind-sets becoming one. And since sex is an act of passion, sex in dreams will most often reflect the merger of a of a quality or mind-set that we are or ought to be passionate about.

Nina had spent almost her entire life being overweight and having very little self-esteem. One day she finally put her mind to it and joined a professional weight loss plan. After almost a year of hard work and dedication, Nina lost over sixty pounds! To her surprise, she found herself to be the object of catcalls on the street and having to turn down interested suitors. Amidst this newfound admiration, Nina had the above dream. Her dream lover is a tall, beautiful black woman; Nina is white. Very often, when a dream character is a member of a different race than we are, he or she will symbolize a part of our selves that we do not know or that seems "foreign" to us. Nina was certainly unfamiliar with her beautiful side. It was always there; she just kept it private and hidden away on her psychological "back porch." Her dream was showing her that she was getting to know this side of her self and she was "integrating" it into her psyche.

"Sex with a Creature"

I was in some house when all of a sudden this dinosaur comes running out of nowhere. It chases me throughout the house. The next thing I know, I'm in the passenger seat of a car having sex with the dinosaur! My mom is driving and doesn't seem to mind at all.
 - Judy 34, Memphis, Tennessee

61

Yes, this sort of dream will DEFINITELY not only leave us wondering about our sexuality, but about our sanity as well! Again, fear not. This is not as uncommon a dream theme as one might think and, as bizarre as this sort of dream can be, it too is all about the "union" of qualities, ideas or opinions. Since dinosaurs, as well as other various creatures, do not have ideas or opinions, this dream is about taking on and merging with the qualities associated with a dinosaur. Judy's Dino-lover symbolizes something in her life from long ago that she thought was "extinct," but has now come back to "unite" with her.

Judy had wanted to be a mom for as long as she could remember. Growing up she never dreamed of a career for herself because she wanted to pursue the noble profession of Mommy. Shortly after marrying at the age of twenty-four, she had to give up on that dream… at least for a while. She and hubby just couldn't make ends meet and if they were to bring a child into the world Judy couldn't afford to give up her job. As far as she was concerned, if she couldn't raise her child, no one could! After ten years of scrimping and saving and hard work, hubby finally got a decent promotion and the idea of being a mom, which had "died off" long ago and was all but "extinct," became a reality again. Judy's mother makes an appearance in this dream. She symbolizes Judy's own maternal instinct, which is now "the driving force" in her life and is pleased with her union.

"Husband Having an Affair"

"Affair dreams" are also about uniting with a quality, opinion or behavior… BUT, to the dreamer it is an unwelcome union! We may dream our spouse is cheating when we feel he or she has taken on a behavior or attitude that is taking away from the marriage. In such instances the subconscious mind feels "betrayed" and will respond with an affair dream in order to get our attention so that we will deal with the matter at hand.

I dreamed my husband was having an affair. I know he's not cheating in real life because his office is in the house and we are very happily married. In the dream I went to the hotel they had been meeting at to confront them. I caught a glimpse of the back of "the other woman" right before I woke up. She was wearing a huge sun hat and had a big lizard tail! - Maurine 35, Cheektowaga, New York

Even though Maurine's hubby is as faithful as a Labrador, her subconscious mind does not see it that way. It feels "betrayed" by his new golf buddies. Maureen and her husband had just moved to a new town, so when her husband befriended some men in the neighborhood who also had an interest in golf, Maureen was actually happy for him. That is, until he spent all his free time with his new friends and adopted their silly slang as his own and used it a little too often. Maureen didn't want to burst his bubble and therefore became very lonely. Her dreaming mind then intervened and said, "He may as well be having an affair! You need to do something!"

Her motivation in this dream was to confront her husband. In her attempt to do so she was able to see "the other woman," the thing that was taking away from the marriage. The message from this dream lies in what she saw. The giant sun hat indicates something is being covered up – Maureen kept her loneliness "under wraps." Backs and tails are both things that are "behind" us and will often symbolize the past. Lizard lady is letting Maureen know that she needs to confront hubby so that the issue can be put "behind" them and made like the lizards of long ago... "extinct."

"Wife Having an Affair"

I had a feeling my wife was cheating on me so I hid behind the bedroom door. When she and the "other man" came in to the room, I leaped out from behind the door and started cutting their hair. – Robert 42, Wausau, Wisconsin

Robert's dream also reflects his unhappiness with something his wife had "united" into her life... the idea of getting a job. Robert and his wife married and had their son at a fairly young age. She had spent her entire adult life raising their son and now that he had gone off to college, she was bored. Robert, being a bit old fashioned, did not like the idea of his wife working, especially since they did not need the money. This dream not only shows his desire to "cut that idea short" (remember, hair symbolizes thoughts and ideas), it also shows that if Robert were to impose his desires on his wife, it might come across as a hostile action.

"Adultery Dreams as an Aphrodisiac"

My husband and I were living in a house surrounded by woods. I was outside looking for him. I found him in the woods having sex with this tall, blonde, pretty woman.
- Tina 27, Spartanburg, South Carolina

Naturally, Tina was afraid that it meant she should not trust her husband. On the contrary, this dream was actually giving her some good advice. Sometimes our dream weaver will give us an adultery dream so that we will make sure we keep the fires of passion burning in our marriage.

Tina had the above dream right after she got married. Woods in dreams symbolize mystery and the unknown. Tina's marriage, like all new marriages, is surrounded by mystery. They have yet to discover all the habits and behaviors (good and bad) that are still unknown to each other. In the dream she is searching for her husband, indicating that she is still exploring who he really is. What she finds is hubby in the thralls of passion with a blond babe! That blond babe is Tina. She represents Tina's alluring, passionate side. She is attractive so that Tina will be attracted to this element of her own personality. This dream is showing Tina that, in this new marriage, she is not only discovering her husband but she is also discovering her erotic temptress self.

Have you been having some spicy dreams lately? Perhaps you've got a mystery man or woman that keeps popping into your dreams. Or maybe you've been uniting with a family member, a friend or co-worker in your dreams and it leaves you feeling concerned or disturbed. Whoever it is and whatever the case may be, just be sure to ask yourself what aspect of that person – or thing – would be useful in your life right now. All these forms of unions, dating, marriage sex and adultery, point to something that is missing in your life. So when you get one of these dreams, don't let it worry you... or let it get you too hot and bothered! Just know that there is some integrating that needs to be done or that has been done, and that you are the better for it.

"Nothing contains more of your own work than your dreams! Nothing belongs to you so much! Substance, form, duration, actor, spectator — in these comedies you acts as your complete selves." - Friedrich Nietzsche

Artist: Lauri Quinn Loewenberg   **Medium:** Digital media

Chapter Ten

Star Quality

࿔ঙ৩৲৹৶

"Floating Madonna"

It's late at night and I am floating about a foot above the ground at my parents' house as I always do(in my dreams). I float through the kitchen, through the den and up the stairs into the playroom. Madonna comes out of my bedroom, into the playroom and asks me what I'm doing. We're old friends and she is spending the night with me as if we were teenagers. I try to teach her how to float like I do but I can't seem to get off the ground anymore, however Madonna is able to do it anyway. She floats up and up and up and makes it all the way up to the ceiling! I cheer her on. I am so proud of her!

When a celebrity makes a guest appearance in our dreams, he or she will symbolize our own star quality, our ability to "perform" and shine in life or in a particular situation. Madonna has been a recurring celebrity guest in my dreams for years. She is a very powerful, talented and successful performer. I watched her rise to the top in the eighties and have been intrigued by her perseverance and her staying power. So whenever she makes an appearance in my dreams I know that my dreaming mind is using her to remind me of my own desire and ability to rise to the top.

I had the above dream shortly after a sudden surge in my Dreamology career. All of a sudden, things began to fall into place and my column and my radio interviews were getting noticed! I kinda felt like I actually might be able to "rise to the top," just as I rose to the top of the stairs in my dream and just as Madonna rose to the top in her career. My dream took place in my parents' house because that is where my desire to become successful began. What little girl doesn't dream of being a movie star or a famous ballerina? Madonna emerges from my bedroom into my playroom, symbolizing that my "inner star" was coming out to play. She's like an old friend in the dream because she represents a part of myself that I like and am happy with. My dream is showing me that my own personal Madonna, my determination and ability to "perform," will allow me to reach heights I didn't think were possible. I just needed to believe in myself and be my own cheerleader.

Woo HOO!!

"Bono and Princess Diana on a Giant Slide"

I was in an airport about to catch a plane. In order to board the plane we had to get on this long, winding slide. It just so happens that Princess Diana was in front of me. As we're sliding down the slide I catch a glimpse of my reflection in a window. I am Bono from the rock group U2! I raise my arms in the air and let out a "Woo Hoo!"
- Maureen 31, Greenville, South Carolina

Princess Diana and Bono are both aspects of Maureen's personality that are ready to "take off." They are both known for their charity, and therefore symbolize Maureen's caring and giving side. Maureen annually donated money to her local homeless shelter and rather than throwing out her old clothes or household items she would donate them to Goodwill. But that wasn't enough for Maureen. Deep down she wanted to do more. After years of intention (though never following through), she finally signed up to volunteer at a hospice in her area, caring for the terminally ill. That very night she had her dream of Bono and Princess Diana. Maureen was following the charitable Princess Diana's lead, sliding "deep down" into her psyche where her desire to actively give of herself waits for her to board. On the way down, she sees herself as Bono. Her flamboyant, cause-fighter self had emerged and was ready to "perform." Maureen was happy with her reflection in the dream because her subconscious mind was very happy with Maureen!

"Drinking Conan O'Brien's Milk"

Conan O'Brien and I were in his kitchen and I was drinking all his milk, glass after glass. I kept telling him not to worry because I would buy him another gallon. After drinking the first glass I saw a black slimy blob in the bottom of the glass. I didn't care so I filled the glass again and gulped it down. - Randy 26, Spartanburg, South Carolina

Conan O'Brien is a late night comedian. Milk represents nourishment. In Randy's dream he is drinking all of Conan's milk indicating that he is "drinking in" a sense of humor. Randy had his dream after his wife of three years left him. Randy was in an awful lot of pain and was kept up "late at night" by his emptiness. He was "thirsty" for the emotional nourishment he was no longer getting and to fill the void he became the comedian of his social circle. He got plenty of laughs but something was still amiss. The slimy black blob in the bottom of the glass was letting him know that there's still some negativity in his life that he mustn't ignore. Randy's dream was teaching him that yes, humor can heal us, but usually not nurture us.

"Mick Jagger's and Keith Richards' Sweet Lovin'"

My wife and I were making love. Suddenly, we turned into Mick Jagger and Keith Richards of The Rolling Stones and continued making love all the while! - Mark 38, Memphis, Tennessee

Sex in dreams, as discussed in chapter nine, is all about a union of qualities or opinions. Mark's dream, as bizarre as it was for him to experience, is simply showing him that the union he has with his wife has the "harmony" and stamina to last a long, long time. Just like Mick Jagger and Keith Richards, Mark and his wife have the ability to make beautiful music together. "Ti-yi-yi-yime is on their side, yes it is."

"Pregnant Howard Stern"

Wow! I must really be drunk!

I was at a party trying to walk down a staircase but I kept stumbling. I figured that I had drank too much. When I got to the bottom of the staircase I stumbled again and bumped into Howard Stern. Even more to my surprise was that he was pregnant! He was surprised that I was surprised. He told me he had given birth to all his children. – Heather 37, Buffalo, New York

Staircases represent progression either in life, career, or a relationship. Heather is stumbling *down* the staircase, which means she is digressing rather than progressing in some area of her life. Her dream reflects her current situation as she was recently fired from a marketing job. When she reaches the bottom she bumps into shock jock Howard Stern. He represents the source of her current digression. Since Howard is in radio and talks for a living he symbolizes the way Heather communicates. Howard is opinionated, obnoxious, and does not care what people think… and so is Heather, hence her firing. On the flip side, he's funny, successful, and known for destroying his competition, which is why he was pregnant in the dream. He represents the part of Heather that is successful and "gives birth" to new ideas and projects through aggressiveness and "Stern-ness." This part of Heather causes her set backs as often as it "produces" success. This dream was telling her not to worry about her recent set back because something new with great potential (just like a baby) is on its' way into her world!

"The Death of Steve Burns?"

I was in my childhood home when a plane flew just over. Once it reached the other side of the house it crashed. I ran to see if there were any survivors. I saw someone crawl out of the wreckage. I ran to him and to my surprise it was Steve from the children's show "Blue's Clues." I rolled him onto his back and he died right before my eyes. - Sherry 32, Memphis, Tennessee

Sherry is the mother of a little girl who is a big fan of the childrens' show "Blue's Clues." At the time of Sherry's dream Steve Burns, the host, was leaving the show. Sherry's dream reflects what many parents were wondering, "How will my child handle this change?" That's the key word here… change. Death in dreams means change, getting rid of the old to make way for the new. The inquisitive and clueless Steve that Sherry's daughter had come to adore would be no more. Sherry's subconscious mind sees it as a death. She was empathizing with her child's loss. This is why her dreaming mind placed her in her childhood home. (It may not seem like much to concern one's self with, but from a child's perspective it's a big deal. Heck, I remember crying as Mr. Rogers put his dress shoes back on and sang good-bye to me every day!)

"Eating Pickles with Jimi Hendrix"

You gotta try these groovy pickles, man!

I was sitting on railroad tracks eating pickles with Jimi Hendrix.
- Paul 27, Duluth, Minnesota

Sometimes the celebrities in our dreams are symbolic of a particular character that he or she once played or a particular song for which he or she is known. Jimi Hendrix is best known for his song, "Are You Experienced?" That is precisely the question Paul was continually asking himself at the time of his dream. He was in the midst of starting up an alternative newsweekly in Duluth, a project that was as exciting as it was stressful. He often wondered if he was experienced enough to pull it off. Paul's dream was encouraging him by telling him that he's "on the right track." Pickles themselves, or anything that is pickled is preserved. Perhaps Paul's dream was also telling him to take in and preserve those groovy Jimi vibes so that he won't get "side tracked" and then find himself "in a pickle."

"Pamela Anderson's Opinion"

I was trying to catch my hat that had blown off my head. I bumped into Pamela Anderson and she told me that I shouldn't be wearing shorts because my legs were ugly. I tried to come up with an excuse but couldn't. Then I realized my hat was gone. – Marissa 15, Richmond, Virginia

Believe it or not, but Pamela Anderson seems to be showing up in women's dreams more often than in men's! She is the quintessential perfect woman (physically anyway) and this is why so many young women dream about her. Today's media bombards us with gorgeous, thin, chesty babes that happen to make us average gals feel kinda substandard… Hello insecurity! Nice to see you again!

Marissa is at the age where she is trying to find her identity; she is trying to grasp what "hat she will wear" in this life. A doctor, a teacher, a mom, what? In the dream, Pamela tells Marissa that her legs are ugly. Legs symbolize our inner tools that allow us to "move forward" in life and "stand up" for ourselves. Her dream is showing her that her life quest is hindered by her insecurities of not being pretty enough or thin enough. This dream is a warning that if she continues to be distracted by such superficial issues, she will surely lose sight of what she really wants out of life.

"A Sad President Clinton"

I was returning home from work and noticed that there was a large crowd of people in my backyard. I got out of my car and went into the backyard to see what was going on. President Clinton was sitting on my porch. He had his face in his hands and was crying.
– Christopher 48, Baton Rouge, Louisiana

Presidents in dreams reflect our own ability to rule our lives and "preside" over our issues. In Christopher's dream, President Clinton was crying on his back porch. As we learned in chapter eight, back porches point to something in our lives that we wish to keep private and hidden from the view of others. Christopher is a building contractor and "presides" over a crew of twelve men. He had been trying to keep his financial problems on his metaphorical back porch, but they were getting so severe that he was going to have to let some of his men go. Christopher cared deeply for his crew and was grieving inside over the thought of losing some of them. One day one of his crew asked him if there were money issues and that night Christopher had his dream. What he had been trying to keep private was becoming known (the crowd in the backyard). The way President Clinton had his face buried in his hands not only reflects Christopher's sadness but also suggests that Christopher should stop hiding the problem and "face" his employees.

"Boogying with Queen Elizabeth and Prince Charles"

I was at a banquet with Queen Elizabeth and Prince Charles. There was one long table in the center of the room and many people were seated at it. There was a jazz band playing and the Queen was gettin' down and boogyin'! There was a portrait of the Queen on the wall and the Queen in the portrait was dancing too. Prince Charles was angry and embarrassed.
– Gayle 25, Eugene, Oregon

The Queen symbolizes Gayle's powerful feminine characteristics as well as her ability to lead. Gayle was always a leader. She was a debutant, her high school's homecoming queen, and class president. Basically, she was considered to be pretty uppity! Gayle had this dream at a time when she wanted to shake her well-to-do, prim and proper image. There was a fun-loving, party girl inside just waiting to come out. Her dream is telling her to throw caution to the wind, it's time to let her hip, funky, feminine side "rule" her rather than her stuffy, crumpet-eating, masculine side. The dancing portrait is a reflection of how Gayle wants the world to "picture" her – respectable yet down-with-that. Keep up the fancy footwork, sister friend!

"Ringo Starr Explodes"

I was late for school even though I haven't been in school for over twenty years. I ran up the stairs and into the lobby. There was a crowd of people and police tape everywhere. I fought my way through the crowd to try to see what had happened. I made it up to the front and to my horror I see that Ringo Starr had exploded! - Carol 43, Boston, Massachusetts

Carol's dream seams awfully disturbing when, in fact, it is commenting on a very exciting situation. Carol had this dream the night her boyfriend proposed to her. The dreaming mind will sometimes use a celebrity's name as a pun. In Carol's dream Ringo Starr symbolizes her engagement ring (a diamond is a "star" placed on a ring). The explosive fate that poor Ringo met in this dream is actually Carol's "burst" of emotion. Most of her friends had been married for quite some time, which is why Carol's dream began with her being late. She had been waiting a long, long time for Mr. Right!

'The Wise Robert De Niro"

I was walking down a path with an older gentleman. The background was sort of like ancient ruins entangled with vines. I was asking him questions, all the questions I ever wanted answers to. He answered but I can't remember anything he told me. We came to the end of the path and I finally saw his face... It was Robert De Niro! He then reached into his pocket, pulled out my eyeglasses and tossed them at me. - Montrelle 26, Phoenix, Arizona

Montrelle's subconscious cast Robert De Niro in the role of Montrelle's older, wiser self in this dream. De Niro symbolizes the aspect of Montrelle's personality that guides him down his chosen path in life because De Niro is someone Montrelle aspires to be like, wise with age, confident, and complete in his trade. All those overgrown, entangled vines are actually questions, issues and problems that Montrelle needs to "straighten out" before they over-run his path, his direction in life. His dream is letting him know that all the answers have been with him all along, he merely needs to "open his eyes" to that fact and then "focus" on what is important... It will all become "clear" to him sooner or later.

"Roger Ebert's Pancakes"

I was making pancakes for Roger Ebert, the famous movie critic. As I was taking them to the table they fell off the plate. I picked them up off the floor and found that they had black, curly hair all over them! I picked the hair off and served them to him anyway. - Ashley 30, Toronto, Canada

Ashley had this dream after receiving a poor evaluation at her place of work. She was clearly feeling heavily "criticized." The pancakes that fell on the floor reflect her hopes of receiving a good evaluation – they "fell flat." But her dream is revealing why she received the evaluation she did; she is careless at work. Like cleaning schmutz off the pancakes rather than making a fresh batch, Ashley would do what was easiest for Ashley. Naughty, naughty!

"Tom Brokaw's Underwater Newscast"

I was watching Tom Brokaw on the evening news. He was at his desk as usual but everything was underwater! His words were gargled. It was driving me crazy because I couldn't understand anything he was saying! - Mike 38, Cookeville, Tennessee

Tom Brokaw delivers the latest news and happenings of the world to us each night, so in Mike's dream he symbolizes information, something Mike needs to know. But notice how Mike can't understand what is being said. When we get dreams like this, where it's hard to make out what someone is saying, it could very well mean that we aren't listening closely enough to those around us.

At the time of this dream Mike's wife was very unhappy in the marriage. She had been trying to get him to go to counseling but he refused. Mike felt his wife was being overly emotional and he continually dismissed her pleas. The water in Mike's dream is the most important symbol. Remember, water is the emotional realm, and in Mike's dream it is the barrier between him and the information he needs to hear. Rather than seeing his wife as having something informative to say, he saw her as an overly emotional woman. He was allowing his wife's emotions to "drown" the message she wanted to "broadcast" to him.

"Kissing Whitney Houston"

Whitney Houston came to my home for dinner. We began to sing "The Greatest Love of All." She then took my hand and started to walk with me to my bedroom while still singing. I am not a lesbian but for some reason Whitney and I just started to kiss. Then she jumped up and ran out of the room still singing. - Vallerie 38, New Haven, Connecticut

Once again we have a song defining a celebrity. Songs are catchy and tend to stick in our heads. They are powerful forms of expression and our dreaming minds will use them to convey messages to us. "The Greatest Love of All" is an anthem of confidence. It's all about loving and appreciating the beauty within the self and passing on that awareness to our children. This type of narcissism is a hard thing to come by these days and Vallerie, like so many of us gals, has a rather serious narcissistic deficiency. Whitney Houston came over to dinner because self-love is something Vallerie "hungers" for. Kisses often symbolize an initiation into a new form of awareness but it can also symbolize verbal expression. Whitney's kiss is urging Vallerie to realize her own inner beauty. Just as Whitney ran out of the room still singing so should Vallerie croon to the world about her new realization. Once we are able to love and appreciate ourselves, life suddenly becomes much more "harmonious."

What celebrities have been making guest appearances in your dreams lately? What stands out the most about each celebrity? Is it a particular quality, a song or a role he or she has played? Perhaps the message is in the celebrity's name. Pay attention to what your dream celebrity is doing and saying. The way he or she acts in your dream reflects the way you are "performing" or the way you *need* to perform in waking life. The qualities you associate with each celebrity just might be qualities YOU possess. Your star- studded dreams are telling you that you too are a star in your own right. As you venture down the red carpet of life, keep your head held high and let your inner star shine!

ಬಃಀಀ

"Cherish your visions and your dreams as they are the children of your soul; the blue prints of your ultimate achievements."   - Napoleon Hill

Artist: Lauri Quinn Loeweberg   **Medium:** Digital media

Chapter Eleven

A Bun in the Oven

ഔ൯ഌ

"Baby in a Glass Box"

My husband I are walking, hand in hand, in an enormous field of lush, green grass. Vines are twisting and curling their way along this vibrant green carpet as far as the eye can see. The tiniest little buds are just beginning to pop up along the vines, promising to bear either fruit or flower. I don't know which. Suddenly, we come across a glass box about the size of a dishwasher. Inside the box sits a perfect, beautiful baby. I reach inside and ... I wake up.

I look at the clock. It's only five in the morning. This is the day I was planning on taking a pregnancy test. Well, I don't think I'll be able to go back to sleep knowing what momentous task awaits me so I clamber out of bed and take the test… two blue lines. I'm pregnant!

Looking back, I now realize that my dream was telling me what the little white stick had confirmed later that morning. Instead of blue lines, it told me in images. The field is symbolic of the opportunity for growth. The vines, which seemed to have no beginning or end, represent my family line. The little buds reflect the state of the pregnancy at that point. And the glass box is the womb. It is glass because it would become "clear" to me that a baby was indeed inside.

During pregnancy women will dream more because we are sleeping more and our hormonal levels are changing. While pregnant, our dreams will reflect the journey we take with our unborn child from conception to birth. Sometimes our dreams will clue us in to the fact that we have conceived before our waking mind knows it, such as the dream above. Throughout our pregnancy the symbols in our dreams change as the fetus, our body and our emotional balance changes. This chapter not only focuses on the dreams of mommy-to-be but of daddy-to-be as well, for he too has dreams that are reflective of his hopes and anxieties about what the future holds.

First Trimester

(weeks 1 – 12)

During the first few weeks of pregnancy the body, as well as the mind, is adjusting to the new little visitor inside. Lots of dreams involving rapidly growing objects happen at this time because this is when the embryo develops the most, going from a one celled organism into a three inch long human with a head, arms, legs and even a beating heart! Dreaming of intruders in the home is not uncommon as it reflects feelings of being "invaded" by a foreign object. It is also common to have dreams of fruits, flowers and other vegetation, which are caused by the awareness of fertility and the ability to "bear fruit." Small water-dwelling creatures such as frogs, tadpoles, fish and turtles are probably the most common dream symbol at this time as they mimic the tiny water-dwelling creature inside the womb.

"Baby Seal in a Garage"

I opened the door leading to my garage. It was empty except for a baby seal. I just so happened to have some raw fish in my refrigerator so I put it on a paper plate and placed it on the floor of the garage. As the baby seal ate it he began to grow and grow until he filled up the entire garage! - Jamie 26, Little Rock, Arkansas

Jamie had this dream before she knew she was pregnant, although her body knew and was sending signals to her subconscious mind courtesy of her hormones. The garage is a fairly common symbol for the uterus. It holds and protects our car until we are ready to leave and in the same way, the uterus holds and protects a fetus until it is ready to leave. The baby seal in Jamie's dream is letting her know that "the deal is sealed," because there is in fact a baby in there. She also conveniently had some raw fish on hand to feed the baby seal. Jamie's pregnant body was conveniently equipped with the appropriate tools to nourish her unborn child. The baby seal grew and grew until it filled up the entire garage just as Jamie's embryo would grow and grow until it would fill her entire uterus.

"Frog in a Purse"

I was searching everywhere for my purse. I finally found it because a strange noise was coming from inside it. I opened it up and there was a gigantic frog inside! I remember feeling so proud of the fact that I had a frog in my purse.
- Andrea 41, Greenville, South Carolina

In Andrea's dream, she is searching for her purse. Searching for a purse or wallet (as discussed in chapter four) is a classic dream reflecting one's need to discover his or her own identity, value and credibility because that is where we keep our money, credit cards, and I.D. But when the body is pregnant, the dreaming mind will then see the purse (or even a pocket) as a metaphor for the uterus; perhaps this comes from the kangaroo! Inside Andrea's purse is a frog, which symbolizes the small water-dwelling critter that is within her womb. No wonder Andrea was so proud of her frog! After a lifetime of searching and struggling to discover her true self, she finally found her identity… as Mommy!

"Boiling Milk"

My wife was boiling milk in a saucepan on the stove. I came into the kitchen to say hello to her but it scared her and she spilled the boiling milk onto her chest and stomach.
– Hector 28, Silver Springs, Maryland

Ah, the dream of a man who just found out he's going to be a daddy! Hector's wife is boiling milk because she is the one "cooking up" the baby and also because she is the one that will be producing the milk. As excited as Hector was about the future, he was also afraid of the harm it might due to his wife's body. Notice how the boiling milk spilled onto her chest and stomach, the two places that will be affected the most by the pregnancy. That's a major concern for many, many men. It's kinda hard to witness the body he has become so fond of and comfortable with being stretched to a seemingly impossible state of affairs!

"Turtle Ice Cream"

I was eating a bowl of vanilla ice cream with chocolate syrup and lots of little turtles.
- Ted 31, Baton Rouge, Louisiana

While Hector's dream reflects a future father's fears, Ted's dream reflects a future father's excitement! Ice cream is made of milk (obviously a recurring theme in the expectant parents, dreams) but it is also a treat to eat! And turtles are not only symbolic of the embryo; they also symbolize patience. Clearly, Ted could not wait until he could "gobble up" that "sweet" little baby.

Second Trimester
(Weeks 13 - 24)

In the second trimester, one third of all dreams will refer to the baby. That is because the body and the mind have finally adjusted and accepted their little passenger. It is also because within this particular trimester, the body begins to show. There's no denying it now! Common dreams at this time include having a see-through belly! Ultra sounds are given during this trimester and the baby is actually seen. "Hubby-having-an-affair" is also a frequent dream theme. Mom-to-be is becoming concerned she is no longer attractive to her mate due to her growing belly. It is also common to dream of miscarrying or premature birthing as the reality of labor and delivery sets in. Those dreams are merely indicative of anxiety, not harbingers of things to come.

"See-through Belly"

I could see inside my belly. Instead of a fetus there was a turtle and he was running on a hamster wheel! - Rose 29, Boston, Massachusetts

What mom-to-be hasn't wished she had a womb with a view so she could check on the progress of her little bundle? Rose's subconscious gave her this dream to assure her that everything is going just fine. The turtle is not only showing her that slow but sure progress is being made but it is also showing her that her baby, like a turtle, is well protected. The hamster wheel indicates that even though Rose may sometimes feel her pregnancy is going nowhere, the wheels are indeed turning. This dream is telling Rose to be patient and relax while you've got the time; they don't make hamster wheels big enough on which babies can tire themselves!

"Premature Delivery"

I was lying in bed feeling my baby move inside my belly. Suddenly, he begins moving frantically from side to side. I can feel him move down into my pelvis. I call to my husband that I think I am in labor. He pops right out. There is no pain at all! But he is very, very small, pink and skinny. I hold him to my chest to keep him warm and tell my husband to call 911.
- Melissa 30, Roanoke, Virginia

Melissa's dream is a very common one among pregnant women, especially once they hit the second trimester. Losing the baby is the biggest fear of all and is often expressed while dreaming. This sort of dream is also the way the psyche prepares itself for the arrival of such a fragile and helpless little soul.

"Giving Birth to a Talking Baby"

I was lying on my bed in my parents' house. I am in labor and about to give birth. My older sister is there to help me deliver the baby. The baby comes out in one push with absolutely no pain at all and to my surprise, is laughing and talking! - Jill 28, Germantown, Tennessee

Giving birth to a talking or older child is more common with first time moms. Perhaps it is because an older child seems less threatening than a helpless newborn. These dreams are also caused by impatience, an emotion we have already encountered several times in this chapter! In Jill's dream, her baby is not only talking but also laughing, which reflects her hopes of an intelligent and happy child. Jill's sister is a helpful character in this dream because she had already given birth to two children. And notice how both Jill's and Melissa's dreams involve a quick and easy delivery with no pain at all. This is yet another hallmark of a first time mom's dream caused by the hopes of an easy delivery, as well as the lack of understanding of what the labor and delivery process truly is.

As the reality of parenthood sets in, mom-to-be is most often dreaming about the baby, while dad-to-be is most often dreaming about how his life is going to change…

I'm in an abandoned building in my old hometown. I'm protecting and hiding my brother from a futuristic military. My brother, who is outgoing, independent, and very successful in reality, was hysterical and extremely depressed. I'm embracing him and trying to comfort him with supporting words.   - Steve 26, King of Prussia, Pennsylvania

Steve's dreaming mind is using his (childless) brother as a representation of Steve's own carefree, outgoing, independent self. He is aware that this part of his life is in danger. The futuristic military is Steve's own realization that he is going to have to live a more strict and disciplined life in the very near future. As his focus turns from having fun to familial responsibilities, the family from whence he came comes to mind. His dreaming mind placed him in an abandoned building in his old hometown to remind him of his own parents. Steve had not been in touch with them as often as he knew he should. His dream was reminding him that since he was going to be a parent soon, he'd best not abandon his.

αβ∞∝

Third Trimester
(Weeks 25 – birth)

 During the final stretch of pregnancy, large or oddly shaped buildings are prevalent in a pregnant woman's dreams symbolizing a now large abdomen and fetus. Difficulty driving a bus or other large vehicle reflects the difficulty she may have maneuvering her very pregnant body. Dreaming of rain and floods points to anticipation of the amniotic sac breaking.   Dreaming of death is fairly common as mom-to-be ponders the cycle of life and subconsciously realizes that her life, as she now knows it, is dying off. The pregnant woman will also find herself dreaming of her own mother an awful lot as her psyche prepares for its' new role as "Mommy."

"Two Sons"

It was pouring rain outside. I came into a house I've never seen before. There was a little boy sitting on the edge of a toddler bed. Beside him, against the wall, was another boy covered up and sound asleep with his back to me. I sat down with the "awake boy" and asked him why he was still awake because it seemed late. He handed me a stethoscope that he had fashioned out of construction paper. I took the stethoscope and used it to try to hear his heartbeat. I was very disappointed that I couldn't hear one.   – Jody 24, El Cajon, California

 Jody was concerned that this dream pointed to either a miscarriage or perhaps even a twin she was not aware of being inside her. In fact, this dream merely reflects the duality of Jody's relationship with her unborn son. The "awake boy" is the son she has named, the son she talks to, sings to and fantasizes about playing games with and teaching to count. That is the boy Jody has created a relationship with. The boy under the covers with his back to her is the mysterious aspect of her baby. He symbolizes what is yet to be revealed to Jody, which is why he's covered and not facing her. Notice how she points out to the "awake boy" that it is late... it is "late" in Jody's pregnancy. He is on the side of the bed, indicating he is just about ready to come out of his warm snuggly womb. Beds are often symbolic of the uterus because throughout pregnancy the fetus is somewhat at rest, and is safe, snug, and bundled up. The construction paper stethoscope reflects Jody's hopes that her son might "construct" his life after his father's who is a medic in the Navy. Her main concern from this dream is that she was unable to hear the child's heartbeat through the stethoscope. That is a common fear-based dream occurrence showing up and overriding the fact that the stethoscope was only paper and not likely to work anyway! All this takes place in an unfamiliar house, which symbolizes the unfamiliar mind-set of being a mom that she will soon "move into." Entering that state of mind takes the act of giving birth, which is what the pouring rain represents, the gush of amniotic fluid that occurs upon the beginning of motherhood.

"The Milk Machine"

I was sitting on my bed with my mother. She told me that in order to be able to breastfeed I had to hook myself up to this machine first. It looked like a garden hose attached to this huge seven-foot tall glass tank. I attached the hose to my breast and the tank began filling with milk. When it was filled I noticed that there were worms and bugs and things floating around in there. I was horrified in the dream but when I woke up, I actually felt a little better about the thought of breastfeeding. – Kim 27, Springfield, Ohio

Anxiety over breastfeeding is another common issue, especially in the third trimester, which brings about some rather interesting dreams. Kim had decided in the very beginning of her pregnancy that she was going to breastfeed. As her due date approached, she began to read up on all the ins and outs of breastfeeding.

The above dream is actually helping Kim to cope with her decision. After learning what to expect from breastfeeding, Kim's subconscious equated her role as a ready-on-demand nursing mother to that of a big ol' milk machine. Her mother appears in this dream as a helpful figure. A pregnant woman's mother is a frequent guest in her dreams because the mother is usually the model for which she will pattern herself as a mom, not to mention that the mother will be on the receiving end of an array of novice questions from "Why won't he stop crying?" to "How do I get peanut butter out of her hair?" Basically, Kim's dreaming mind is using her mother to show her that educating herself on the subject has allowed her to "get all the bugs out" of her anxieties over what is truly a beautiful and nurturing experience.

"Out of Control Car"

My husband, some friends and I were in our car. My husband and I were in the back seat and a friend was driving at high speeds through lots of traffic. We told her to slow down but she didn't seem to be able to control her speed. She was zigzagging between cars and around bends in the road. I was just crying in the back seat, scared to death. - Nathalie 22, Ottawa, Ontario

Feeling out of control in the last trimester is not at all unusual. At this point in the pregnancy the body has stretched beyond comprehension and is no longer easy to "steer." The pregnant woman also has no control over when the baby will come... it will happen when it happens! This is one reason Nathalie found herself in the backseat of her car, reflecting every woman's fear of not making it to the hospital in time and delivering in the backseat! Nathalie's friend and her friend's husband symbolize another element of her life that is out of control, Nathalie's irresponsible self. Nathalie and her husband had made a habit of going out with these two particular friends rather than dealing with more important things that needed to be done. Her dream is warning her that she had been letting her irresponsible side be her "driving force" long enough. At a time when Nathalie is feeling so out of control, she may as well "take the wheel" of something she can control and start being more responsible.

"Delivering Kittens"

Look honey, a bouncing baby kitten!

My wife and I were in my childhood bedroom and she went into labor. There was no one around to help so I had to play midwife. Well, she gave birth to a litter of kittens. They all died but one.

– Michael 28, Chattanooga, Tennessee

Michael's dream reflects many of the classic anxieties expectant fathers around the world share as the due date approaches. His dream takes place in his childhood bedroom because deep down he is not sure he is mature enough to be responsible for the upbringing of another person. Delivering the baby himself points to apprehension over the labor and delivery process; Michael's also unsure of what to expect and WHEN to expect it. While dreaming of cute and cuddly animals is common in the last trimester of pregnancy for both expectant parents, Michael dreamed his wife delivered a litter of kittens because his first and only experience of the birthing process was when he watched the family cat deliver a litter when he was just a boy. All the kittens die except one because Michael's dreaming mind is reassuring him that he will have only one precious little bunchkin to be responsible for, not an entire litter!

These short nine months are a magical time for expectant parents, in waking life as well as in dreaming life. Dreams at this time are rich with vivid and bizarre imagery, imagery that can sometimes be quite disturbing and seemingly very real. It is important to remember that no matter how disturbing the dream may be, it does not mean there is or will be something wrong with your pregnancy. Dreams are simply visual metaphors for the uncertainty and excitement both mommy and daddy are experiencing. Now more than ever is the time to pay attention to your dreams and to write them down. Sharing your dreams with each other is a wonderful way to come together and open up about your feelings. Discuss the scary dreams and realize that they are perfectly normal and are simply telling you that you're a bit too anxious. Laugh about the funny dreams and know that they are showing you have a good, healthy attitude about the pregnancy. You'll have a great time and you just might learn something new about each other - and yourself!

"Then thou scarest me with dreams, and terrifiest me through vision." – Job VII : 14

Artist: Michael Quinn   **Medium:** Color pencil/Digital media

Chapter Twelve

Nightmares, The Dark Side of Dreaming!

ᔒᏣᏴᏣ

"Night of the Zombies"

It is a warm summer night and I am walking down the driveway towards my house. I step into a puddle of water. As I check to see how badly I've dirtied my shoe, the puddle begins to ripple and slowly morph into a zombie. It is green, moldy and swampy looking. I run into my house, lock the door, and then run into the kitchen to call for help. There is water in the sink. It too slowly turns into a zombie. It climbs out of the sink and begins to chase me. I run through the dining room and as soon as I pass by the air conditioner I hear a "poof." I turn around and see a green, slimy splatter all over the floor. Apparently, cold air kills these things! I hear footsteps behind me. It must be the zombie from outside! I spin around, grab him by the shoulders and try to muscle him in front of the air conditioner. I notice green slime oozing from the corners of his mouth. As we struggle he begins to change into a blond, young man. "Do I really want to kill this thing?" I ask myself. Just then I accidentally step into the splatter of goo that was previously the zombie from the sink. It once again turns into a zombie. I wake up with my heart pounding!

That is the calling card of a nightmare, when we're suddenly propelled into the waking state by the rapid and forceful beating of our own heart… and sometimes our own screams! The body does not know the difference between a dream and an actual waking event, therefore it reacts the same as it would in a real life traumatic situation. The dreaming mind takes advantage of this adrenaline pumped response because we are more likely to remember the dream that caused us to awaken so dramatically, and we are also more likely to try to figure out the meaning behind it. The scarier the dream is, the more important the message. My nightmare certainly got my attention! And the message it had for me was extremely important!

Zombies are popular subjects for horror flicks as well as for nightmares. They are the living dead, the *un*-dead, someone who will not die. So when these guys staggered into my dream, I knew it meant I had to deal with some unfinished business. At the time of this dream, The Dream Zone was a 900 number that was not doing so well. In fact, it was pretty much "dead." We had trained, certified dream analysts on stand by, ready to help people understand his or her strange dreams and nightmares. Unfortunately at that time, the psychic phone lines were giving 900 services a bad name. My husband, and my partner/teacher (Dr. Katia Romanoff) and I had tried everything to turn it into a "thriving" business but it was quite clear that this thing was going to die. It was a very upsetting reality for all three of us because we knew that The Dream Zone was something that could truly help people; it was something that *everybody* could relate to because everybody dreams. Well, my subconscious wanted to make sure I did not let The Dream Zone die so it brought it back to life in my dreams.

The small bodies of water that the zombies came from symbolize the creative "juices' or waters that give birth to all projects and ideas. The first body of water was a puddle formed by the rain or metaphoric tears the three of us shed over the death of The Dream Zone. The second body of water was in the sink, which means The Dream Zone needed to undergo a cleansing in order to be reborn. But in order for this project to become what it was meant to be, it had to get my attention so it chased me down! Notice how the cold air could kill the zombies. My dreaming mind was showing me that if I got "cold feet" or put this project in "cold storage" it would indeed die off. That's why my dreaming mind came at me again with another zombie, one that would show me it was actually a handsome prince inside, not a moldy, squishy, oozing monster! It just needed the right care and attention in order to be transformed into something more pleasing than a 900 number. Very shortly after this dream, The Dream Zone column was born!

"Shadowy Creatures"

I used to dream that I had just woken up in my bed and there were several shadowy creatures or "spies" standing around my bed just looking at me, as if they had some sinister plan and were about to act. I'd become so terrified that I couldn't move or scream. I've had this dream all the way up to my early twenties. Also, if I wake up from the dream, I'm still paralyzed and can't scream, though I'm desperately trying to scream.
- Mike 30, Chattanooga, Tennessee

When we find shadows lurking in our dreams, it usually means there is something "vague" and "obscure" around us or within us that we would rather not bring to the light of day. Mike had this nightmare up until his twenties, during the years he was becoming a man. There were always multiple shadows symbolizing the many nuances of growing up: raging hormones, rebellion, emotional outbursts, insecurity, etc. All those fun things were creeping about Mike's psyche, waiting to pounce when he least suspected it! Ah yes, the good ol' teenage years. Once he reached full maturity, somewhere in his early twenties, the shadows never returned! This is because he learned to acknowledge and integrate some of those shadowy elements into his personality while the others he simply outgrew.

Another interesting aspect to Mike's dream is the "sleep paralysis" he experienced. Little do we know that when we go to sleep and enter the REM (dreaming) stage, the brain stem releases a chemical that actually paralyzes our skeletal muscles; otherwise we would get up and act out our dreams! Sometimes when we wake up suddenly, usually from a nightmare, the brain isn't always able to reactivate our skeletal muscles in time and so we are unable to move for a brief moment. It's a fairly common occurrence and nothing to worry about.

"Driving off a Mountain"

I am driving a car in the mountains on a very curvy road with the ocean to my left side. All of a sudden my car stops running as I am climbing the mountain. I start to roll backwards. I step on the brake only to find out I have no brakes. I am picking up speed and the road is so curvy that there is no way I can steer backwards down this road. I know I am going to run off the road, crash into the ocean and die. I always wake up before I crash. – Donna 58, Perris, California

Losing control of one's car is a classic nightmare for someone who feels he or she has lost control of something that is happening in his or her life. At the time of Donna's nightmare, her husband was trying to overcome a serious drinking problem. Kicking any addiction is "a big mountain to climb." Naturally, Donna wanted to "drive" her husband in the right direction. To a certain degree, she could. But from time to time her husband would slip up and set back his progress, hence the car rolling backwards. This caused Donna to feel that he was "failing her" just as the brakes on the car failed. Speeding down the curvy road reflects Donna's feelings of being in a "downward spiral." Her desire to control this issue was getting no one nowhere… fast! Donna's dreaming mind stepped in and gave her this nightmare to let her know that ultimately, hubby is the only one who can "put on the brakes." And that's just what Donna did. She stepped back and let her husband be the one in control and, last I heard, he's happy and sober!

"Mouth Full of Blood"

I dreamt my mouth started to ache and I tasted blood. I started to worry as more and more blood filled my mouth but I didn't want to swallow it. I couldn't keep the blood in my mouth any longer and it spilled onto the floor in front of me. I noticed shards of teeth in the pool. I began to panic and then I woke up. – Joseph 17, Phoenix, Arizona

Blood… Yeck! It's just as scary to see in a dream as it is in waking life. Blood is the fuel that keeps our motors running, so to the dreaming mind blood means energy. When you see it in a dream or nightmare it's a warning that you've been wasting or losing energy.

In Joseph's nightmare, blood was filling his mouth. As we learned in the "Body Language" chapter, anything having to do with the mouth in dreams points to the way we communicate verbally. Joseph had this nightmare after "spilling" his guts to a girl he had a crush on. Sadly, after "pouring" his heart out to her, she pretty much stomped on it and threw it in the trash. Just like the shards of teeth on the floor, his hopes were shattered. Joseph's nightmare was showing him that he was wasting too much energy wishing he could put those words back in his mouth. There's just no use crying over spilled milk, or in Joseph's case, spilled blood!

"Demon Possession"

I dreamed my daughter was possessed, so we had her exorcised. But as soon as the priest left she was possessed again and went floating down the stairs.
- Shannon 28, West Minister, South Carolina

According to some religions, evil spirits can overtake an innocent and unsuspecting soul. In the same way, materialistic greed, violence and other various outside influences can take hold of us and corrupt us, especially our children! That is what Shannon's nightmare is about. It reflects her fear that her young and impressionable daughter might fall prey to the powers of certain music, video games, commercials and peer pressure that plague our youth today. Shannon is afraid she won't be able to protect her from everything, that even after she helps "save" her from one thing, her daughter will be affected by some other negative influence thus ending up on a downward path (symbolized by her floating down the stairs). Believe it or not this is a fairly common dream these days, indicating that we parents have gotta be vigilant and stay on our toes!

"The Corpse"

I was attending the funeral of an old high school classmate (as far as I know he is still alive and well). All my old classmates were there and we were standing in the back of the church. For some reason the coffin was on the back pew. It slid off the pew and opened up. The body fell out and the legs buckled underneath it. The eyes were all bruised and swollen. We all gasped and turned our heads. - Alison 28, Spartanburg, South Carolina

If you were to actually witness a corpse spilling out of a coffin, you'd probably turn your head and hope to God that someone would put it back in the coffin... ASAP! That's why Alison's dreaming mind used this exact scenario in her nightmare. It was letting her know that something very disturbing, something she thought she had "laid to rest," was revealing itself once again. It was something she needed to "put a lid on"... ASAP!

When Alison was in high school she was very popular and smug. She was often the ringleader when it came to taunting those of "lesser status" than she. The dearly departed classmate in her nightmare often fell victim to her antics. And so he appears in her dream as a reminder from her subconscious that this bad behavior is "spilling" into her life once again. The bruised, swollen, dead eyes and the classmates turning their heads away are hinting that this has to do with avoidance, something Alison would rather not see. This nightmare was telling her to "open her eyes" to this unpleasant behavior and "bury" it once and for all.

"Coffins Coming Out of the Ground"

This nightmare has been recurring since I was a child. I am on a street that I played on all the time when I was young. It is late a night. The streets are empty and the streetlights are really bright except for the fog coming in around them. I am running down the middle of the street. It feels like someone is behind me but I cannot ever see anyone so I keep going. The pace picks up and I am going faster and the fog gets thicker. Then everything around me starts exploding. Coffins start popping out of the ground, cars are being turned over, fire hydrants are spewing water. Then there is a bright light at the end of the street. I know if I get to the light I will be okay. I wake up sweating and shaking. – Donna 36, Bedford, Texas

Donna's nightmare has been recurring almost all of her life because it is commenting on a lifelong behavior pattern. Donna had a tendency to clam up whenever she found herself in a tough situation. She would never let anyone know that she was in a bind or feeling helpless. She always tried to fix the situation all on her own because she did not like to appear weak or needy. This stubbornness did not sit well with her subconscious so it tried to communicate its displeasure through these recurring nightmares.

The fog coming in around the streetlights may merely seem to be an appropriate setting for such a spooky dream when in fact, it actually has a deep meaning! The fog reflects that Donna is in a situation in which she is unable to see clearly. The bright streetlights indicate a desire to "shed some light" on the situation. Donna is also being chased, which we all know by now means she is trying to avoid something in her waking life – she is avoiding asking for help. Notice that the more she runs, the more hostile the dream becomes. This is the nature of dreams; when we continue to ignore the dream or the issue it is commenting on, the dream will become more and more hostile in order to get our attention. The exploding frenzy is a warning that she is suppressing too much. The more she holds back, the more likely she is to "explode" at some point. Things she thought she had "buried away" (the coffins) must be exposed, and her emotions (spewing water) must "vent." The bright light at the end of the street is a bit of encouragement. It is letting her know that there are answers for her and that there is "light at the end of the tunnel." She's just going down the wrong avenue to get there.

"Crawling Out of a Grave"

I dreamed that one of my best friends died and after we buried him he crawled out of the grave. So we buried him again and once again he crawled out. Everyone was screaming and I woke up so scared!
- Jamal 35, Memphis, Tennessee

Again we have the dead coming back to life, a common nightmare theme that is usually a good indication that we need to deal with some unfinished business. In Jamal's nightmare, that unfinished business concerned his best friend. About a year before Jamal had this dream, he found out that his girlfriend and his best friend had had a little fling. His best friend confessed and then the girlfriend left the picture. Jamal and his friend mended fences and all seemed well and good until Jamal got a new girlfriend… and this nightmare! Just as his friend crawled out of the grave, Jamal's distrust of his friend resurfaced. His nightmare was letting him know that this issue still had some life to it. Jamal needed to clear the air with his friend once and for all before either one could "rest in peace."

"Murdering My Boyfriend"

A girl I do not know handed me a dagger and told me to kill my boyfriend. So I took the knife and sliced his neck ever so lightly. I watched the blood drip down his neck. Then I started stabbing him with all of my might. I had so much power and energy I just couldn't stop. I felt his warm blood splashing all over me. I felt the struggle to get the blade through the bones and the flesh. I stopped once he fell. The anonymous girl took the knife and started stabbing me. I felt every single slice and every stab. I could feel my own warm blood all over me. Then I fell down in slow motion until I finally hit the ground. My boyfriend was lying there. He called my name and then it got blindingly bright and I woke up screaming. – Bayleigh 22, Phoenix, Arizona

Whew! That one IS awfully gruesome! But even so, this nightmare is actually trying to help Bayleigh improve her relationship with her boyfriend. Murder in dreams means forcibly "killing off" some aspect of one's life. Bayleigh is murdering her boyfriend, indicating that she is trying to end certain elements of his personality that she does not like. Stabbing, in particular, points to "stabbing remarks" and cruel words that "cut like a knife." All that warm blood splashing around in this dream symbolizes all the energy that is being lost in the relationship (it takes a lot of energy to dish out criticism just as it takes a lot of energy to be on the receiving end of it). And that anonymous girl that manipulated the whole bloody mess is the part of Bayleigh's personality that Bayleigh refuses to acknowledge… the big, bad critic within. It is the part of her that not only doles out the cutting criticism to her boyfriend but also to herself. Long story short, Bayleigh's nightmare is showing her that she's waaay too critical of her boyfriend, and much too hard on herself as well. The bright light at the end of this dream indicates that this harsh behavior is finally "coming to light" and can now be improved.

Terror Attacks Our Dreams

Since the terror attacks on September 11th, 2001, nightmares have been on the rise. These days we all have an underlying sense of anxiety, stress and insecurity, the three major building blocks for nightmares. Below are just a few of the hundreds of nightmares that have been reported to me since that horrible day.

"Dropping the Bomb"

I am riding in a van with two other people. We hear on the radio that Saddam Hussein has just dropped a nuclear bomb. Somehow we know that the explosion will be reaching us in a few minutes so we pull to the side of the road and jump out of the van. My cat is in the van. I call to him but he is scared. He finally jumps out and runs into the traffic. I turn my head so as not to see his fate. I jump over the guardrail and begin to run. As I am running I see inside an apartment window. There are two men sitting there having a conversation. I think to myself, "Those lucky bastards. They have no idea that we're all going to die any minute."
- Heather 30, Macon. Georgia

This nightmare begins as Heather is calmly traveling down the road of life when suddenly she and her companions hear that the bomb has been dropped ("Dropping the bomb" is also a term for really bad news)... yet another dream reflecting how our lives have been interrupted since 9/11/01. They pull over to the side of the road, indicating that Heather feels her life's journey has been "sidetracked." Her cat symbolizes independence and pride (being that they are rather aloof and independent creatures). Heather feels this aspect of her life, of all our lives, is seriously threatened. Those "lucky" unknowing men she sees as she is running from the bomb reflect her wishes that she could escape what she knows and continue on, blissfully unaware of the danger our society faces.

"Exploding Computer"

I was playing games with my son on the PC when suddenly the screen went out and then flashed writing in some foreign language. The PC then exploded and I was caught in a blinding light and heard a ringing in my ears and was unable to find my son. I was trying to call to my wife to get my son but I was unable to move or see anything.
   – Frank 35, Staten Island, New York

The personal computer games symbolize the game of life. Frank, being the concerned and caring parent that he is, is teaching his son the rules of life and how to compete and win in this game. The computer screen goes blank and flashes a foreign language indicating that something that is beyond Frank's understanding (the terror attacks) is suddenly interfering with his "personal" world. Then the PC explodes. Explosions usually mean a burst of pent up frustration may be on the way but they can also mean there is a major shift going on in one's thinking... and these days the latter is usually the case as we are all rethinking our priorities. But for Frank, his shift in thinking was related to the fact that a new child was on the way at a time when he was no longer sure he wanted to bring more children into such a chaotic world. This nightmare is warning Frank not to "lose sight" of the needs of his son who has been drawing burning buildings almost everyday since the terror attacks. It is also urging him to not let the fact that there are some things beyond his control keep him from "moving" forward in life.

"Satan's Mission"

My room was hell and the hallway was the stairway to Heaven. All of these people were going by on their way to Heaven, while I was stuck in this dark room. Satan was in there with me. He was trying to get me riled up over the unfairness of this. We began making plans for a war. I was "enlisted" to go on a mission but I had to be disguised. He started talking about removing my skin and putting something ELSE there. I asked him if it would hurt. He said it wouldn't and that I just needed to relax. I woke up with my heart pounding.
   – Ruschia 27, Hertford, North Carolina

This nightmare reflects Ruschia's struggle to understand the mindset of those that have waged war on the free world. Satan naturally symbolizes the evil forces that manipulate and rile up the minds of those that are easily influenced into becoming terrorists by telling them that they will be able to go to Heaven or "Paradise" if they "fight the infidels." Ruschia is enlisted to go on a mission and her skin is removed just as the terrorists are "stripped" of their independent thinking and are enlisted to go on homicidal missions. After this nightmare, Ruschia decided to take a break from the twenty-four hour news channels.

As frightening as a nightmare can be, it is important to remember that it is actually helping you to solve your problems and overcome your anxieties. When it scares you into attention it is doing its duty. No matter how disturbing the nightmare, try not to view it as something to be ashamed of or to fear. Look at it as an opportunity to improve yourself and better your life.

Whether you're plagued with constant nightmares or you just experience the occasional heart pounding, sweat drenched awakening, *write it down.* Take a good look at the dilemma within the dream. Does it seem like anything you are going through in waking life? If there is a villain, ask yourself if its behavior reminds you of anyone or anything. Finally, imagine that you are in the nightmare again. Now that you can make decisions consciously, what could you do or say to thwart the villain? What action could you take to overcome the desperate situation? Remember, it's a dream so you don't have to abide by the laws of waking life. Be creative! Psychologists and researchers have found that if we can handle the situation in the dream, then we are more likely to overcome the waking issue as well.

అంబరంద

"And he dreamed, and behold a ladder set up on the earth, and the top of it reached to heaven: and behold the angels of God ascending and descending on it." - Genisis 28:12

Artist: Lauri Quinn Loewenberg   **Medium:** Digital media

Chapter Thirteen
Dreams After Death

ॐॐॐॐ

"The Stairway to Heaven"

I am walking arm in arm with my grandfather through a museum. We stop at the bottom of an enormous spiral staircase. Each step is as tall as I am. He turns and looks at me and tells me he must go. "What is it like where you are, Papaw?" I ask him. "Very secure," he answers. "Tell me more!" I plead. I am aware that he has died and is only here for a short visit. There's so much I need to know and so much more of him I want to have. "That's all I can tell you." He begins to grow and grow until he is twenty feet tall! He lifts me up to his chest and gives me the warmest, most loving hug I have ever experienced. He puts me down and begins to climb the staircase. As he walks away, I notice that he is wearing an aquamarine suit. When I awoke the next morning, that dream immediately poured itself into my memory. I felt that loving hug again just as if Papaw were actually right there giving it. I smiled and thought, "Thank you Papaw!"

I had that dream two weeks after my grandfather's death. At that point in my life, my grandfather was the closest person to me that had ever died. After his death I really struggled with my own mortality, with the meaning of life and with just getting by each day. All the exciting things in my life became mundane and all the mundane things in my life became utterly pointless. What was it all for if ultimately... we just die!? I had lost my belief in life after death… until my dream!

The setting of my dream was a museum, a place where the past is preserved. Even though my grandfather is no longer tangible his memories will forever be preserved in my psychological "museum of family history." The enormous spiral staircase symbolizes "the stairway to heaven," the progression from this life to the next. It was so enormous because it is a "big step" to take and the understanding of it is much bigger than I am! My grandfather's message to me was the most important aspect of this dream, that the place he is at is "very secure." He was letting me know, in not so many words, that he was fine. The more I thought about those two words, the more I realized that there were no better words he could've said. He will never be sick again, nothing can ever harm him and he has nothing to fear. He resisted telling me more because, I suppose, I need to find those things out for myself. Before he left my side he grew to be twenty feet tall, not only because his awareness and understanding has "expanded" but also because he will always be a "big" presence in my life. This dream has proven true as it has now been twelve years since he died and I still find myself missing him terribly and wondering what he thinks of the things I have done with my life. He even returned to me recently in a dream the night my sister's husband died and gave me that same big, warm, comforting hug. And as for that aquamarine suit, well, that's my favorite color! It is the color that I believe "suits" me best. Perhaps he was letting me know that the comfort I found in this dream is something I can share with others, that helping others find comfort in his or her own dreams is the "suit" I should wear in this life.

My grandfather was a man of great faith and I believe he truly came to me at a time I needed him most, at a time when I had lost faith. Perhaps my subconscious mind was merely giving me what I needed then, a way to cope. Indeed, our dreams are Mother Nature's tool of choice for this nice handy healing mechanism but we must also ask ourselves if our dreams are not also a means by which those that have passed on can continue to communicate with us.

This chapter will explore both the healing aspect of our dreams after the death of a loved one as well as the possible "contact" aspect of our dreams.

Healing Dreams

After someone we love dies, it seems impossible to continue with our own lives. Overcoming the pain, regret and sense of hopelessness after a death is probably the hardest thing we ever have to do in this life. Paying attention to our dreams during this time is one of the most helpful and healing things we can do for ourselves. Our dreams will not only reflect our healing progress but also offer insight into how we can make these tough days a little easier.

"I Thought You Were Dead"

Just recently my father-in-law died and I have been dreaming about him a lot lately. Either he is still with us and everyone is happy again or we are back by his side when he was dying.
- Joyce 44, Hollister, California

This is a very common dream after losing a loved one. The dreaming mind, which does not understand the passage of time or the loss of a life the way the waking mind does, does not understand why this person is gone. It is grappling with the loss and is a bit confused. When we are asleep and all the doors of our mind come open, our mind will ask and answer its own questions. "Is he alive?" it asks by thinking of the days when our loved one was still with us. Then the inner mind remembers, "No wait. We stood around his bedside and watched him pass away." These are powerful life and death images. Both the conscious mind and the subconscious mind will take awhile to absorb and adjust. In many cases such dreams can show up for years to come. However, the "deathbed" dreams do eventually taper off and the healthy and alive dreams remain as the subconscious realizes that the sickly images are not a healthy thing in which to cling.

"Everyone's Leaving Me"

In the past week I had a close friend die in a car accident. Last night I had a dream that my brother died and then it turned into my boyfriend and then into my little sister and then it turned into a war where we were all going to die. I woke up really sad and devastated, thinking that someone is going to die soon. I am really worried. I don't want to lose anyone else close to me.
- Amy 16, Highland, Utah

This is also a common dream after the death of someone we love, especially for children and young adults that do not have much experience dealing with the permanency of death. The problem is that the inner self, expressed through the dreaming mind, is afraid, truly terrified, that more death is on the way. Somebody died, and now it has to try to understand things like tragedy and needless death. This is a posttraumatic anxiety dream and is NOT a prediction of any further loss. Of course, the hard part is getting the subconscious to believe that. It just takes time trying to understand and heal after a tragic loss. This sort of dream is merely part of the healing process.

"Back From the Forest"

I have had many dreams about my husband since he died. At first, I would dream that he was with me again but he would then fade away as I was screaming his name. Now, almost a year later, I dream that he is not really dead but has just been lost in the woods. When he comes back I am ecstatic, but then realize that he does not really fit into my life anymore. I wonder if he will let me continue to go to church and I am afraid he will be upset with me for selling the house. So many things go through my mind. But all in all the dreams are comforting because they are so real. It is like getting to see him again and again. – Deborah 35, Montgomery, Alabama

Deborah's dreams are showing her that she is definitely making progress in the healing department. Her dreams have gone from her pleading for her husband to stay to her wondering if he's going to disrupt her current life. After her husband died, Deborah joined a church, started her own business and has kept herself active. She has gone from lonely and empty to active and full. She has moved on, which is what we must do after someone we love dies. Deborah's subconscious now realizes that even though she will always miss her husband terribly, his place is no longer with her but in a place that is mysterious and unknown as symbolized by the woods. And his occasional visits are a welcome occurrence that will continue to enrich Deborah's spirit.

"Butterfly Window"

I was sitting on the edge of the cliff where my brother and I used to hang out with our friends up until he died. I was looking up at the starry night sky. There was this window in the sky, just sort of hanging there, and through the window it was daytime and I could see all these butterflies flying around in there. I woke up in awe. It was such a cool dream!
- Naomi 27, Richmond, Virginia

Naomi had this dream about three months after her brother died, and it is a beautiful representation of her healing progress. She is revisiting the hang out spot where she and her brother spent many wonderful moments together. Deep down she knows she can always find a part of her brother there. But on a deeper level, that particular hang out area was a cliff. Cliffs are symbolic of being on the verge of change. If Naomi had been teetering on the edge it would indicate that she is on the verge of losing control and "falling" deeper into depression.

Thankfully, we see Naomi comfortably perched high atop the cliff gazing upon a starry dreamscape. And this dreamscape is revealing to her that she is on the verge of a transformation, of a "new day." Butterflies symbolize one's metamorphosis into a higher form or a higher awareness. Windows symbolize ones perception or "view" of things. Perhaps that new view, that new awareness, is that her brother, like a butterfly, has been transformed into a higher form of existence!

"The Flying Roller Coaster"

My mom, my dad and I were on a landing waiting for a roller coaster. I told my parents that I was NOT willing to ride. My dad told me that we both had to go in order to be with my mom. So, we all climbed in and took off. Just like a roller coaster, we were on a track that wound around and around, up and up. We were facing one direction and my mom's seat was facing us so I was looking straight at her the whole time. Finally, we reached another landing and my dad got out and told me to come with him. I started crying and told him I didn't want to go. I wanted to stay with my mom. He started to help me out and I grabbed the bar in my lap and he had to pry my hands off. Finally he got me out and we waved goodbye to my mom. The roller coaster continued on its track and as we watched, it gained momentum just as it reached the end of the track and was able to take off into the air. – Rachael 29, Franklin, Tennessee

Rachael had this dream five months after losing her mother to a rare lung disease. She was having a hard time accepting her mother's death so her dreaming mind actually took her through that process! Her dream begins as she and her parents are about to board a roller coaster, which is a metaphor for life; it's full of ups and downs. Rachael was unwilling to board because somehow she knew that if they all got on, only she and her dad would get off. She didn't want to separate from her mother. They were all able to ride together for a little while just as they were all able to enjoy life together for what seemed like a short time. Together as a family, they reached certain levels in life, symbolized by the different landings. But then the time came in which they had to go their separate ways. So we see Rachael and her dad reluctantly remain at one level as her mom gets to go on. And notice how the roller coaster continues on without the track, soaring into the air, the spiritual realm! This is how Rachael's dreaming mind is showing her that her mother is no longer chained to the earth; she no longer has limitations or safety bars to hold her down. She is free.

☼ Cg 80 Q

Contact Dreams

While it has yet to be proven, it is widely accepted and believed that our loved ones that have died can contact us through our dreams. If there is life after death and if there is a means by which the dead can still communicate, then it seems only logical that our dreams would be the tool of choice.

If consciousness survives bodily death, then it would still exist as a form of energy, and as science has proven, all energy travels in waves: light waves, sound waves, radio waves, etc. As the human brain works, it produces electrical energy that can be measured in waves. By measuring the frequency or pulse rate of those waves, one can determine the brain's state of consciousness.

As discussed in Chapter One, as we fall asleep, our brain waves slow down. Who's to say that the dreaming state of sleep is not the perfect frequency of brain wave activity that would allow us to "tune in," like a radio, to all those nether-worldly transmissions out there?

The two main characteristics of what are believed to be "contact" dreams are: 1. an interaction between the dreamer and the deceased and 2. a sense of joy or calm that is felt upon waking. These dreams are often life changing, or at the very least reaffirming in one's belief in an afterlife. Read on and decide for yourself...

"The Breath of Life"

I had a dream my husband was back in the hospice in the process of dying. He appeared disheveled and very sickly. The doctor said that he needed some help to breathe. I inhaled while he exhaled into me. When we both realized what we were doing we burst out laughing. I felt a sense of joy! In fact, I woke up very happy. – Darlene 53, Dahlonega, Georgia

This was the first dream Darlene had about her husband since he died of cancer fifteen months earlier. She wanted desperately to dream of him all that time but was unable to. Sometimes ones' ability to cope with the grief can be so delicate that the subconscious mind may temporarily block certain dreams – or at least the memory of them – until it feels the time is right, emotionally.

Darlene's dream placed her and her ailing husband back in the hospice where he had spent his final days, indicating she is still emotionally and psychologically stuck there. This is not uncommon for a grieving dreamer, who had to watch a loved one waste away and ultimately die in a hospital or in hospice care. It takes a while to get the image of the loved one's weakened state out of the conscious mind as well as the subconscious mind. The doctor in this dream is actually Darlene's own inner healer. It knows that if she were able to heal the sickly image of her husband, she in turn would be able to heal herself. So she begins to give her husband *mouth-to-mouth resuscitation but rather than Darlene breathing into him, he breathes into her!* That is because s*he* is the one that needs that healing energy, that healing breath. Since her husband's death, Darlene had barely been living and had barely been *breathing*. They burst out laughing because the healing process had begun. Perhaps Darlene's husband came to her in this dream because he knew exactly what she needed. Laughter *is* the best medicine, after all!

"Healthy Again"

My grandfather died recently and I have been having several dreams about him. In one of them, I am in my grandfather's hospital room. He is lying on the bed, dead. All of a sudden, he sits up, swings his legs to the side of the bed and says, "I want to get out of here." His body goes back to its normal, healthy state right before our very eyes. I am ecstatic! I run to the lobby to tell my parents. - Tina 18, Wilmington, North Carolina

It is believed that those that have passed on will make contact with the living (through our dreams) in order to let us know that he or she is okay and still exists. Tina's dream is an example of one of the many ways the dead will convey that message. Her grandfather comes back to life and becomes healthy and normal right before her eyes as if to say, "Hey, stop thinking of me as a dead body. I am alive! I feel great! I want out of this train of thought of yours. This is not who I am!"

"It Happened in a Flash"

I was alone on the beach at night watching the ocean. Suddenly, lightning flashed and there was a figure on the water, floating towards me. His arms were crossed on his chest. He had long blond hair that whipped around his head with the wind. As he got closer I could see that it was my son who was killed in a motorcycle accident two months ago. He stepped off the water and walked on the sand to me. His feet kicked up sand but didn't leave any footprints. He smiled and touched my forehead with his fingertips. It tingled. He then wrapped his arms around me and hugged me tight. I could feel his heart beating, yet I couldn't hear it inside of him.
- Joan 49, Lafayette, Louisiana

Beaches are often the setting when we dream of a loved one that has passed on. The beach is where the sky (the spiritual realm), the water (the emotional realm), and the land (the earthly realm) all meet. We struggle with all three of these things after such a great loss. We struggle with the idea that there could be a spiritual existence after this life. Our emotions are at "high tide," and we struggle with the fact that we are stuck here on earth without our loved one. All these things were true for Joan after losing her son in a motorcycle accident. But after this dream, she actually felt closer to him than ever.

Joan saw her son after a flash of lightning. Lightning bolts are sudden, forceful and powerful energy, which comes from the heavens down to the earth. Therefore it is a common element found in "contact dreams." Notice how her son leaves no footprints on the sand. This is because the laws of physics and gravity no longer apply to him. He is no longer bound by the physical world. Then he touches Joan's forehead and it tingles. The forehead is the place of the third-eye, the place of intuition, foresight and enlightenment. It's almost as if he is awakening an intuitive knowledge within her, the knowledge of an afterlife perhaps. And once again, we have a warm and loving hug. Hugs are a way we come together and express our love for one another on this physical plane. It's interesting how a physical act can seem to cross dimensions! Perhaps it is because it is not the hug, but the emotion behind the hug, that seems to penetrate time and space. When he hugs her, Joan could feel his heart beating but couldn't hear it. His heart goes on (to quote a very famous movie song) yet he no longer needs that biological machine to keep it going. His feelings and his love continues despite the lack of a physical body.

"An Important Phone Call"

I dreamed that the phone was ringing and upon answering it I heard a baby on the line. I kept saying, "Hello? Hello?" The next thing I heard was the theme song from Winnie the Pooh.
- Gina 36, Scottsdale, Arizona

Whenever a phone rings in a dream it means there is an important message for us that we need to pay attention to. When Gina answered the phone in her dream, she heard music and a little baby. Gina lost her baby girl when she was only forty-three days old. At such a young age, her little girl had not learned how to communicate verbally. Naturally she would use something from a musical toy or music box to communicate, something Gina would've played while holding her, feeding her and bonding with her. They say music is the language of the soul... and surely souls don't need words to communicate with one another.

"Lunch with Dad"

I was having lunch with two friends at a table for four when all of a sudden my late father came up behind me and whispered in my ear that he was ready for us to go have lunch together. I looked to my right and saw his face. He had not shaved. I was so glad to see him and looked at him so that I could memorize his face. The way his hair receded, his smile. I then turned to my friends and told them that I had to go be with my dad. – Anna 30, Dallas, Texas

"Contact" dreams can happen even decades after the person has died. Anna's father died in 1979, yet she still has dreams, like the one above, where she believes he is actually communicating with her. She will get these dreams whenever she feels certain areas of her life are empty, like the fourth chair at the table. Anna had lots of friends but still "hungered" for the emotional nourishment of a male companion, which is why her dream took place in a restaurant. She was beginning to worry that she would never find "Mr. Right." So her father comes to her *right* side (sometimes we gals, subconsciously, want Mr. Right to be like our dad). Anna's father takes her to lunch because he wants her to know that she is not empty. He is always with her. And whenever she needs some comfort or guidance, he's always willing to give her a little heavenly push in the right direction.

Have you been dreaming about a deceased loved one? Did you find comfort in those dreams? Did those dreams change your opinion of life after death? Were you given a message in those dreams? Whether our dreams are a means of communication between this world and the next or whether they are simply a coping mechanism after the death of a loved one, they are certainly an important element of the healing process.

If someone you love has died recently, pay attention to your dreams and write them down, even if the dreams are disturbing. They are there to help you come to terms with your loss. Our dreaming mind understands things on a much higher level than the waking mind and will guide us down the road of recovery. It will give us dreams that will not only bring a great deal of comfort but also bring us closer to the loved ones we thought were gone forever. The dreams I had after my grandfather died not only brought me comfort but also showed me that I now have an angel I know.

೩ಞೞಬಎ

"We are near awakening when we dream that we dream."   - Baron Friedrich von Hardenberg

Artist: Lauri Quinn Loewenberg   **Medium:** Color pencil/Digital media

Chapter Fourteen
Lucid Dreaming

෨൚ൠ൚ൣ

"Soaring Over the Ocean"

I am standing on a pier watching the ocean. There is an outdoor café behind me. No one is there except for the waiter. I notice that the waves are gigantic... far too big to be real. Hey, I must be dreaming! Okay, what should I do now? I close my eyes, jump into the air and SOAR! Swoosh! Straight up! I wasn't even sure if I could get airborne. I'm afraid to open my eyes for fear that I will wake up. So I open one eye and look down. I am in awe at the sight of the tiny trees far below me. I close my eye again and just feel myself soar through the air, the cool wind against my face, my clothes whipping against my body. This seems so real. Suddenly, I feel myself become heavy. I open my eyes. I am losing altitude. I feel the mattress on my back. No! Don't wake up yet! Just a little longer! Too late. I'm awake and in my bed. Darn it!

This was my very first lucid dream and when I woke up I was in absolute euphoria! It was so real and, unlike my usual dreams, I had been completely aware and in control of what was going on. I knew I was in an altered state where I had no limitations. I was the writer, director and star of my dream production and it would unfold any way I chose. As far as I was concerned, it was better than sex! Okay, maybe not better but it was a very close second!

Lucid dreaming is when one is aware that he or she is dreaming while still in the midst of the dream. This ability comes naturally and frequently to some while others, like myself, have to work very hard at it and only get to enjoy the experience on rare occasions. Lucid dreaming is a very powerful tool for self-discovery. Once you realize that you are in the midst of a dream you can ask anything and do anything. It's like having your very own genie in a bottle. You can go on a date with your favorite celebrity, you can ride a magic carpet to Paris, write a sonnet with Shakespeare and most importantly, you can ask your dreaming mind to give you guidance or direction in regards to any pressing matters at hand. Lucidity is a doorway to a world that was once unattainable and unimaginable; a world where wisdom and enlightenment wait to be discovered and where your wildest fantasies wait to be explored.

"I Force Myself to Wake up"

Whenever I am having a bad dream where I am being chased or attacked or I see something bad happening to my girlfriend, I'll suddenly realize I'm dreaming and I'll force myself to wake up. – Brent 22, Paris, Texas

Most of the people I have dealt with that have experienced lucidity use this state of consciousness only to wake themselves from a disturbing dream. They do not realize that, rather than simply escape an undesirable situation, they could actually change the scenario completely. For example, Brent could change himself into a rock star and his pursuers into adoring fans who want to praise him and get his autograph. Or more importantly, he could simply turn to his pursuers and ask, "Who are you and what do you want from me?" At which point his hostile dream characters would turn into something benign and reveal to him what issue in his life they symbolize. This is a powerful technique used by many lucid dreamers who want to gain insight and solutions from their dreams. While changing a dream scenario will counteract the message the subconscious mind intended to give the dreamer, it can be fun and give one a sense of power, which may be precisely what the dreamer needs in his or her life at that time.

"The Elevator Ride"

I am riding in an elevator that is going down. It keeps going down for a long time. When it finally stops the doors open and I step out into a beautiful field. I look behind me and see that I have just come out of a tree. At this point I realize that I am dreaming. Everything is suddenly so vivid, bright and rich with color. It's almost surreal! I look down and I am wearing a brown robe like a monk. I look up at the sky and the clouds and the leaves on the trees and everything is so brilliant and beautiful. I want to see more of this place so I decide to float up. It's such an amazing feeling! When I reach the top of the tree I stop myself from rising and sit down on a branch. Just over the hill I can see my elementary school playground. Suddenly, I feel myself waking up so I focus on the swing set. After a moment I am back in the dream and decide to float over to the playground and have some fun. I softly land in a swing and begin swinging back and forth, higher and higher. I am having a great time and I swing so high that I find myself in outer space! Everything around me, the stars, the planets, is so vivid that I wake myself up saying, "Aaaahhh."

- Jacqueline 28, Buffalo, New York

To go down in an elevator, a flight of stairs or an escalator in a dream most often points to something going in the wrong direction, a project, a relationship, self-esteem, etc. But considering the content and nature of Jacqueline's dream, we can be assured that it does not point to any of the above. The downward direction is symbolic of her consciousness traveling down through all the layers of her mind until it reaches its destination somewhere deep within her subconscious. Once there, her dream elevator opens up to reveal a beautiful landscape, a beautiful place deep within Jacqueline's psyche. Notice how she becomes aware she is dreaming after realizing the elevator she was in is actually a tree! It is little incongruities like this that will cause the dreamer to realize, "This can't be so! I must be dreaming!" Suddenly, Jacqueline's dreamscape becomes alive with color and detail because she has realized she is in an altered state of consciousness. Her dream world that surrounds her may not necessarily be any different than in her usual dreams, she just happens to know she is in dreamland this time and she is paying close attention.

Jacqueline notices she is wearing a monk's robe, which indicates this may be a spiritual experience (many who have experienced lucid dreaming believe they have actually left their bodies and entered a spiritual realm, a place not unlike heaven). Trees are also spiritual symbols mimicking one who is rooted here on earth but continually reaching upwards towards the heavens, towards a higher awareness. Realizing she is in this altered reality, Jacqueline decides to float up and perch herself on top of the tree where she then sees her elementary school playground in the distance. Dr. Stephen LaBerge of the Sleep Research Center at Stanford University in California equates lucid dreaming to "having a personal laboratory or playground for trying out new behaviors and ways of being." On some level, Jacqueline realizes her very own personal playground from which she can experiment and learn, like a school, lies just before her.

Notice that when Jacqueline begins to feel her self wake up she focuses on an object, the swing set, until she is securely back within her dream. This is a popular technique used by frequent lucid dreamers. Focusing on an object such as your hand or a building will anchor your state of consciousness and keep you in your dream a bit longer. After successfully anchoring her self in her dream, Jacqueline floats over to the swing set and swings higher and higher until she finds herself floating in outer space. Flying and floating are the most common feats that are conquered in the lucid state. Deep down we all desire to elevate ourselves to a higher level intellectually, spiritually and emotionally. And when we find ourselves in an existential state where anything we desire is possible, one of the first things that comes to mind is to go up, to defy gravity and the laws of the universe, to have complete and absolute control over something that simply can't be. Harnessing that power, if only in our dreams, gives us that spiritual and emotional "high." It expands our minds and our perception of our abilities. Perhaps it was Jacqueline's elevated spirits that seemingly propelled her into outer space or perhaps it was her dreaming mind trying to show Jacqueline her unrealized potential. Whatever the case may be, Jacqueline is a far more open-minded individual since this dream experience.

"Window of Lucidity"

I was looking into a full-length mirror in a white room. As I looked at it, I realized it had turned into a window so I walked through it. I then realized that I was dreaming, and knowing this I knew that I could control it. I met an old man that told me I was one of the few to reach this level of consciousness. He told me that usually only creative thinkers, artists, inventors, etc. make it in and that a lot of inventions are built here first because there is no danger of explosions or injury. Once you're here you can do most anything you want. After that I ran into a friend of mine. We went into a room that had a wall full of small movie screens. There were several people sitting in there watching. You could re-call your subconscious by watching the right screen. My friend stayed behind and I went on. I wanted to find more things to do.
   - Barry 37, Richmond, Virginia

Notice how the mirror in Barry's dream turns into a window. What an appropriate entry into lucidity it is! Mirrors are very much like dreams in that they are reflections of our thoughts and feelings. And windows allow us to view the world around us. Barry's dream, symbolized by the mirror, is allowing him to view his dream world from a new perspective… from a lucid perspective!

Barry takes a very wise approach to his lucidity. Rather than change his surroundings, he explores what this dreamscape has in store for him. He meets an old man who is actually his own older and wiser self. His wiser self reveals to him that he has entered a place, a state of consciousness, where wonderful inventions and works of art are created. Although we all have access to it, it is the artists and inventors that tend to utilize this state of mind the most. For example, Thomas Edison used to keep a cot in his laboratory so that he could, "grab ideas from space."

And finally, Barry runs into a friend and together they find a room full of movie screens. His friend is not playing himself, he symbolizes the part of Barry's inner mind that he likes and enjoys. Who better to accompany him as he reviews various life experiences? The movie screens are an excellent metaphor for the subconscious mind, which records our entire lives, including all thoughts, emotions and experiences and will replay them in our dreams when necessary. In the usual dreaming state, we are at the mercy of the choices made by our subconscious mind, yet in the lucid dreaming state we are able to consciously choose the life experience we would like to review. Barry's conscious mind took an intellectual advantage of his psychological playground and, no doubt, he awoke with great insight!

Most often, lucidity happens during the early morning dream, the longest of all the dreams dreamt throughout the night. It is during this dream that we are closest to awakening and have already gone through the deep stages of sleep. At this point, the mind can much more easily be awake and asleep at the same time. It is hard to comprehend the idea of being awake and asleep at the same time but clearly it is achievable. Lucid dreaming is a mysterious and awesome experience. It not only opens the door to an entirely new awareness of existence, it also hints at the untapped and unrecognized potential of the human brain!

If you've never had a lucid dream experience, fear not! It is very possible to teach yourself to lucid dream. The first step is to start *paying attention* to everything around you. Look closely at the fibers in your carpet, study the wood grain in your door, take notice of all the pores and freckles on your skin. Noticing the details of the things around you in waking life will also help you to notice the details of the things around you in your dreaming life. And attention to odd details in a dream is what will likely trigger lucidity.

As you do this through out the day, ask yourself, "Am I dreaming?" Of course, you're not dreaming but once you get in the habit of asking this question while noticing small details, you are very likely to do the same thing while you actually are dreaming and *that* is what will bring about lucidity. Be consistent. It may happen in just a few nights, it may take a few months. You can do it! You can *wake up* in your dreams.

ഔൟ൫ൕൈ

"Dreams are illustrations from the book your soul is writing about you." - Marsha Norman

Artist: Lauri Quinn Loewenberg **Medium:** Digital media

Chapter Fifteen
Dream On

ॐ❦ॐ❦

There is that brief moment in time, just before waking, when what we perceive as reality begins to melt away and our conscious awareness rises to the surface. It is in that moment that we realize, either with great relief or disappointment, that it was only a dream! How unfortunate that so many of us then disregard the night's experiences as insignificant and jump out of bed to start the day, allowing that magical life we inhabited only moments before to quickly slip away unnoticed.

It is not *only* a dream; it is a world of information, guidance, and insight. It is our wiser self communicating with us, helping us to solve problems and showing us our selves and our lives from a different perspective. Dreams are very real and very much a part of our lives. Would we but allow ourselves to linger in that moment before fully waking, we would be able to capture that dream experience for good and, wow, what a powerful tool for self discovery and self improvement we would have at our fingertips! The magical key that unlocks this power is very simple: *Write down your dreams!*

Keep a notebook and pen or tape recorder next to your bed so that you can immediately record anything you remember before it fades away (dreaming takes place in the same part of the brain where short term memory is stored so you gotta capture those dreams right away!). Seeing these objects every night before you go to sleep will remind your subconscious that you want to remember your dreams.

When you wake up in the morning, don't immediately jump out of bed and start your day. Give yourself two to five minutes to let the dream come back to you. Set your alarm two minutes earlier if you have to. Keeping your eyes closed and staying in the position you slept in helps your body stay connected to your dreaming mind.

As you lie in bed, begin going through the names of all the people you know and the things you do on a daily basis. Since dreams parallel our daily lives, chances are you dreamed about one of these people or activities. As they cross your mind they just might trigger a dream.

Start your Dream Journal. In the beginning, you may only remember bits and pieces of your dreams. WRITE IT DOWN! Even if it seems insignificant or too small of a piece, it is important information. By writing it down you are not only acknowledging your dream, but you are exercising your "dream muscle." The more you do these exercises the stronger your "dream muscle" will become, and the more dreams you will remember in time.

Throughout the day certain things and people can trigger a part of your dream. Immediately write down what you remember and what triggered the memory, or tell someone what you remember. Telling someone your dream helps to imbed it into your memory and can often bring about more details you had forgotten.

Before you know it, you'll be remembering entire dreams, even several dreams a night. If you don't have time in the morning to write down the entire dream just jot down notes that you can understand when you do have the time. Just be sure to go over it in your head a couple of times so you don't forget the details!

Title your dream as if it were a movie. Sum up the whole dream in one line. This is the first step in understanding what your dream means. This will also make it easier to go back and find a particular dream again.

Record any feelings you had when you woke from the dream. Record what you did during that day, any movies or TV shows you watched, people you saw. This will help you make connections between your daily life and your dreaming life.

Every couple of weeks go back through your dream journal and re-read your dreams. Sometimes they make more sense later down the road. By re-reading your dreams you will begin to notice patterns and progressions. You'll discover that you have your very own dream symbols that continue to pop up. As you continue to keep track of your daily events along with your dreaming events, you'll soon figure out exactly what those recurring symbols mean to you. For example, fish are a big dream symbol for me. I know that whenever they appear in my dreams, they are commenting on my creative ideas. When my creative ideas are thriving, my dream fish are thriving and usually multiplying. When I'm having a mental block, my dream fish are usually in peril and I am trying to save them.

You'll soon discover that you've been living a rich and exciting life while you've been sleeping! As your dreams become an important part of your life, you'll look forward to going to bed every night to find out in what adventures your dreams will place you. You'll even look forward to writing your dreams down and you'll marvel at how they will suddenly, magically, make an awful lot of sense to you.

Your dreams are a gift *from* yourself *to* yourself. Their wisdom is ancient, yet their meanings are mysterious. The more you work with your dreams the more your dreams will work *for* you!

Glossary of Dream Symbols

ക്കുള്ളേക

This glossary of dream symbols was designed to be used as a continual reference that will aid you in your dream working. All the symbols in this glossary can be found throughout the dreams that are in this book. After each symbol is the page number(s) where you can read that particular symbol in an actual dream. Each symbol will not necessarily hold the same meaning for everybody. The meanings in this glossary are the most common meanings for each symbol and should help you realize the true meaning for you. Happy dreamworking!

For more information or to schedule a consultation with the author go to:
www.thedreamzone.com

A

Adultery/Affair: (p.62, 63) Is your loved one doing too much of something that takes away from the relationship? Your subconscious mind may see it as a "mistress" or another man.

Airplane: (p.45, 46) Your ability to take off, soar to new heights and reach your goals. If your dream airplane is crashing, could mean you fear something in your life or within you may come crashing down around you.

Airport: (p.66) You are in a place in your life where something is about to "take off" and soar to new heights.

Air Conditioner: (p.81, 82) Cool it. Calm down.

Alien: (p.55) Symbolizes something you are unfamiliar with, something you have never encountered before.

Animals: (p.33) Symbolize our basic instincts and behaviors. Are you behaving or do you need to behave like the animal in your dream? What characteristics does that animal have?

Aquarium: (p.22) Contained emotions or creative juices. Are the fish in your aquarium thriving or dying? You always want your dream aquarium full of clear water and thriving fish.

Arm: (p.25) the way you express yourself and/or reach out to others. Your ability to do something. Could be pun on "arm yourself."

Arm pit: (p.14) May symbolize something you find offensive.

Attic: (p.52) Place where you store your higher and spiritual ideals.

B

Back Porch: (p.69) Houses symbolize the self, therefore porches symbolize extensions of the self. A back porch may mean you are extending yourself in a private, obscure manner.

Back seat: (p.78, 79) You are not in control of some area of your life, you always want to be in the driver's seat in your dreams.

Back: (p.28, 29) Your strength, your ability to carry a heavy burden. Can also mean you need to or you have put something behind you, turn your back on something/someone.

Bar/Pub: (p.15, 58) A need to relax, let go of inhibitions

Backyard: (p. 53) Symbolizes things you like to keep private, away from the prying eyes of others.

Bathroom: (p.13, 19, 54) A need to cleanse oneself of negativity.

Basement: (p.55) Place where you store memories, attitudes, behaviors, etc. that you would like to forget about, that you keep below the surface. Can sometimes symbolize the past.

Beach: (p.96) May mean you need to take a break and relax. On a deeper level, could symbolize your own power; the tremendous energy of the ocean, the land and the sky all coming together.

Bed: (p.10, 38) You may need more rest. May be commenting on private, intimate matters. Is something keeping you up at night? Your dream may even be commenting on your dreaming life.

Bedroom: (p.13, 38) You may need more rest. May be commenting on private, intimate matters. Is something keeping you up at night? Your dream may even be commenting on your dreaming life.

Bedroom (childhood): (p.65, 79) Often points to the beginnings of your hopes, ideals, fears, etc. Where you began your identity.

Bird: (p.9) Your ability to soar, to break free.

Black: (p.66) Mysterious, unknown, can sometimes symbolize negativity

Blood: (p.83, 87) Your energy, your life force, that which keeps you going. If you see a lot of blood in your dream then you are wasting or losing energy or someone or something is draining your energy.

Bones: (p.23) Something you need to bury for good and stop bringing up.

Breasts: (p.28) Femininity, nurturing abilities and instincts.

Bridge: (p.36, 37) transition, getting from point A to point B. Are you trying to cross over into some new area of your life?

Bomb: (p.87, 88) You may be on the verge of an emotional explosion. Can symbolize bad news, "Dropping the bomb."

Briefcase: (p.16) May be pointing to an issue at work. Can also be a pun on, "keep it brief."

Brother: (p.57, 77) What qualities does your brother have? Do you need to utilize those qualities in your own life?

Bugs: (p.7, 78) It's time to deal with something that is "bugging you."

Bury: (p.86) Ask yourself, "Do I need to bury this issue and move on?" "Is this issue dead to me?"

Bus: (p.19) One of the slowest means of getting from point A to point B. Are things going slowly for you? Can also symbolize conforming, going along with the masses. If missing a bus, you may be missing an opportunity in waking life.

Butterfly: (p.19, 93,94) Transformation. Just as a caterpillar changes into a butterfly, you are changing into a higher form or a higher awareness.

C

Car: (p.20, 46, 78) Shows how you are traveling through life or through a particular situation. A speeding car is a good indication you need to slow down and take it easy in waking life. A car with no brakes means you are having difficulty putting the brakes on something. A crashing car may indicate you are headed for a crash, a rude awakening. An out of control car means you have lost control of something in your life. A car that won't start indicates you are having trouble getting things up and running. It's always good to be in the driver seat of your car, it means you are in control.

Cat: (p.36, 87, 88) Often symbolizes your feminine, intuitive energy. Can also point to independence, fickleness, cleverness, pride, aloofness, balance, cattiness or any other traits you might associate with a cat.

CD-Rom: (p.28, 29) Information or ability to process information.

Celebrities: (p.65) Your ability to shine and perform. What the celebrity is doing in the dream may reflect how you are acting in life or in a particular situation. What is your dream celebrity best known for, what qualities do you associate with that celebrity? Perhaps it is a dong they sing or a role they play. If you applied those qualities to yourself would you shine in life?

Chair: (p.36, 37) Take a load off, relax, sit for a spell or get up off your bum and get moving (depending on context of the dream). Could also symbolize your place in the world, where you sit in this life and your view of things

Chandelier: (p.22, 23) Your beautiful inner light, your ability to shine and be grand and graceful. Could mean a grand idea.

Cheese: (p.16,17) Learn to smile more often (say cheese!). As with all food in dreams, could symbolize something you hunger for emotionally, spiritually or physically.

Childhood Home: (p.22, 23, 50) Your ideas, behaviors (good and bad) that began there. Could mean a need or desire to be taken care of just like you were back then. May indicate you are behaving childishly. Could be a reminder NOT to behave as you did back then nor to treat others as you were treated then.

Circus: (p.37) You may be feeling that your life is a three ring circus, there's too much going on. Could also be telling you to recapture your childhood, look at life with the same awe and wonder you looked at a circus.

Class Room/School: (p.14) Time to learn a lesson or educate yourself on certain matters. You may be feeling tested or that you need to pass a particular situation with flying colors. Do you have a fear of failure? If searching for a class you are directionless in some area of your life. If you are late for class you are afraid of missing an opportunity or are feeling unprepared.

Clothing: (p.13, 34, 44) Your attitude or behavior you put on to show the world. Shopping for clothes indicates a need or desire to get a new attitude or behavior pattern. Changing clothes would mean a change in attitude. Cleaning clothes would mean you need to clean up your attitude. Pay attention to the type of clothing and condition of the clothing. Does it reflect your current attitude? Do you need to put on that attitude?

Clown: (p.16) You may be clowning around too much. Could also mean you need to learn to laugh at yourself and the world around you, don't take things so seriously.

Coffin: (p.85, 86) The ending of a situation, case closed. Can also symbolize some issue that needs to buried.

Computer: (p.88) How are you computing certain information?

Computer Game: (p.88) The game of life. How well are you playing?

Cooking: (p.38) Cooking up ideas and schemes, something is in the works. Can also show up in pregnant women's dreams.

Corpse/Dead Body: (p.23, 53, 85) Symbolizes something that is or should no longer be an issue, something that is no longer of any use, something that should be buried and left alone.

Crystals: (p.21) Clarity, crystal clear. Also symbolizes positive energy and spirituality.

Cut/Sever: (p.38) Desire or need to cut someone or something out of your life, a separation. Can also point to cutting painful remarks, cuts like a knife.

D

Dance: (p.58, 59, 69) Dancing around an issue, or moving in harmony with someone or something. Can symbolize joy and celebration.

Date: (p.58) Courting an idea. Uniting with the qualities you associate with your date.

Death: (p.9) Change, the old dying off in order to make way for the new. The end of an issue or relationship.

Demon Possession: (p.84) A negative force that seems to have taken over someone's mode of thinking.

Devil/Satan: (p.87, 88) An evil/negative force. Something around you or within you that tempts you to do the wrong thing, to blame others and be naughty. Could be a warning to clean up your act.

Dinosaur: (p.61, 62) Something from the past that needs to be made extinct.

Digging: (p.23) A form of searching. Dig deeper into the issue. Maybe you are being too nosy. Can reflect a fear of something from your past being dug up.

Doctor: (p.28, 29) Time for emotional, spiritual or physical healing. The part of you that knows what's good for you. Your ability to heal yourself or a particular situation. Pay attention to the advice your dream doctor gives you.

Dog: (p.35) Loyalty, companionship. Could symbolize responsibility, as pets are responsibilities. Could symbolize a fear if you are afraid of dogs. May also symbolize your need or desire to buckle down and train yourself to behave. Look at the type of dog in your dream. What is that type of dog known for?

    German Shepherd: Best known for being a guard dog or police dog. Are you being or do you need to be guarded when it comes to a particular issue? Are you overly protective?

    Husky: Best known as a sled dog. Are you carrying a heavy burden? Are you dragging an issue on too long?

Drinking: (p.66) The need or desire to drink in someone's or something's energy or qualities. To thirst for knowledge.

Drunk/Intoxicated: (p.66) You may not be seeing things clearly. The need or desire to numb yourself.

E

Earthquake: (p.9) You may be feeling that you are in an unstable or shaky situation. Shaking things up. Can also mean a major shift in your life.

Eat: (p.9, 35, 68) To take in spiritual, intellectual or emotional nourishment. Take a good look at what you ate in your dream. If you ate something unusual, then you may have a hunger to take in a particular quality that you associate with that thing. Could be pointing to your diet.

Elevator: (p.16, 100) Movin' on up to the next level. Progression or digression depending on whether the elevator is going up or down. Elevate your mind and spirit.

Explosion/Blowing Up: (p.54, 55, 69, 85, 86, 88) Emotional outbursts. A warning you are headed for an explosion. A huge idea. Sometimes we'll dream of explosions when there is a major shift going on in our lives.

Eyes: (p.85) Open your eyes and take a closer look at your situation. Your perception or point of view.

Eye Glasses: (p.70) Focus your attention. Look closer.

F

Face: (p.27, 59) Face the issue, face the past, face the facts, etc. If there is no face then it may mean you are afraid to face something or it may symbolize a part of yourself that you do not recognize.

Falling: (p.8, 51) Fear of failure, of losing status or of losing control.

Festival: (p.21) Time to celebrate and reward yourself for a job well done. A call to bring out your carefree, fun loving self.

Field: (p.73) Enormous potential for growth

Finding: (p.21, 22, 23) Discovering your unknown or unrealized abilities and talents. A call to look inward and see what you will find.

Fish: (p.22, 34) Symbolizes something you want to catch, keep and nurture, or take in. Can often symbolize creative or spiritual ideas. A symbol for Christianity. A common symbol in pregnant women's dreams.

Fishing: (p.42, 43) Searching for something, trying to get something you want, looking for Mr. or Ms. Right.

Fist: (p.43) Power, strength, ability to fight for yourself and your rights

Fleeing/Being chased: (p.7, 8, 52) Running from an issue. Afraid of confrontation

Floating: (p.10, 65) Ability to rise above the ordinary or to rise above a tough situation. If floating and can't get down could be your subconscious telling you to come back down to Earth, ground yourself, stop hanging around, etc.

Flowers: (p.7, 54) Joy, happiness. Something that can bloom, grow and bring joy.
    Gladiolas: (p.7, 54) A pun on glad

Fly: (p.9) Ability to break free from Earthly woes, things that bring you down and make you feel heavy, ability to soar to new heights. Can be a pat on the back from your subconscious for doing a good job.

Fog: (p.85, 86) Inability to see things clearly. An unclear or cloudy idea or situation.

Forest: (p.63, 93) The mysterious, the unknown. Can't see the forest for all the trees.

Freeway: (p.10) The road of life. The condition of the freeway will reflect the traffic conditions in your life; very busy and congested, slow going, smooth sailing, etc.

Freezer: (p.25) Frozen emotions or ideas. A cold person. Putting some issue in cold storage.

Friend: (p.65, 102) Can sometimes be playing themselves or can symbolize a particular quality the two of you share. Can also symbolize a part of yourself that you like.

Frog: (p.34, 74) Are you leaping into something before looking both ways? A common symbol in pregnant women's dreams.

Funeral: (p.85) Time to put old ideas, attitudes, behaviors or issues to rest and move on.

G

Gallery/Museum: (p.89) A display of all your gifts and talents. A reminder to preserve your memories.

Girl: (p.87) Usually symbolizes your childlike carefree self. Immature, naïve self.

Glass: (p.44, 73) Fragile, easily hurt. Can also mean something is clear to you know. Ability to see through a situation.

Grandfather: (p.51) Wiser, more mature, masculine parts of self. Could symbolize passage of time or old, out dated attitudes and behaviors. If you dream of your grandfather that has died, it may actually be a contact dream!

Grandmother: (p.15, 35) Wiser, more mature feminine parts of self. A need to be pampered and spoiled. Could symbolize passage of time or old, out dated attitudes and behaviors. If you dream of your grandmother that has died, it may actually be a contact dream!

Grave: (p.86) Could be pun on a grave situation. Often indicates you have buried some issue. You don't want to see anything coming out of that grave as that would mean old, dead issues are rising to the surface again.

Grocery Store: (p.16, 17) Your inner storehouse of emotional, spiritual and intellectual nourishment. It is time to access the tools you need nurture and nourish yourself and those around you.

Gum: (p.26) A sticky situation. Chew on this. Something you may need to spit out.

Guts: (p.28) Gut feeling. Spill your guts.

H

Hair: (p.13, 27) Thoughts and ideas because, like hair, it comes from the head.

Hair Cut: (p.28, 63) Cut your ideas short. A change in thinking.

Hand: (p.37) It's in your hands now. Lend a hand. Ask for a helping hand. Also a means of expressing yourself.

Hat: (p.7, 68) Cover up or hide your thoughts and ideas. Could also symbolize the role you choose to play in this life

Head: (p.36) Use your head. Your intellect, your thinking. Strong headed.

Heaven: (p.88, 89) A goal, perfection, your highest ideals, enlightenment.

Hell: (p.88, 89) May symbolize a very difficult time you are having to go through. Fears, anxieties, feeling trapped. An evil force.

Hiding: (p.77) A good indication you are avoiding an issue, you are afraid of confrontation.

Hiking: (p.21) A means of reaching your goals, of climbing higher.

Hometown: (p.77) A reminder not to forget where you came from as well as a way to measure how far you have come.

Homosexual Affair: (p.61) Admiring your own femininity or masculinity. Being proud of your gender.

House: (p.49,50, 51, 52) You, your state of mind, the dwelling place of your soul. The state of the house reflects your state of mind.
> **Mansion:** Could symbolize your goals. Grand ideas. An elaborate way of thinking and doing.
> **New House:** A new way of thinking and behaving
> **Old House:** Old, out of date attitudes. An old soul. If the house is run down, you may be feeling tired and run down.
> **Under Construction:** Rebuilding yourself, you are undergoing renovation, transformation.

I

Ice Cream: (p.75) Time to treat yourself.

Invisible: (p.25, 58, 59) Whatever is invisible in your dream is missing, not acknowledged or not utilized in your waking life.

J

Jar: (p.39) You are holding things in, keeping things bottled up.

Junk Yard: (p.53) Discarded, unused and negative ideas, attitudes and behaviors. Can also symbolize the past.

K

Kitchen: (p.54, 55) A place of preparation. Cooking up ideas and schemes. A hunger for emotional, intellectual or spiritual nourishment.

Kitten: (p.36, 37, 79) Sexuality, sex kitten. Can also symbolize your playful, young self.

Kissing: (p.71) Anything having to do with the mouth points to verbal expression. Kissing often means communicating. Sometimes signifies an initiation or a betrayal.

Knife: (p.87) A need or desire to cut or sever ties, to separate yourself from a particular issue or cut out a particular behavior, idea or attitude. Harsh, cutting remarks, cuts like a knife.

L

Laughter: (p.95) Joy, happiness. Laughter is the best medicine. Don't take things so seriously.

Leg: (28, 29, 68) Strength. Your ability to stand up for yourself and move forward.

Lightning: (p.96) A flash of inspiration. A sudden and bright idea. A huge burst of energy. Sometimes a spiritual symbol as it comes from the heavens.

Lights: (p.85, 86) Time to shed light on a situation. Knowledge.

Lion: (p.37, 39) Courage, bravery. It may be time to roar, show who is king of the jungle.

Lip Stick: (p.8) Draws attention to the mouth therefore point to verbal communication. Is there something that needs to be said? Lip service. Could also be a pun on make up.

Lose/Lost: (p.19, 20) Nothing lasts forever. Learn to appreciate what you have. Perhaps you need to let go of something. You may be feeling that something is missing from your life. Fear of losing control.

Lunch: (p.97) Hungry for fellowship or for emotional, spiritual or intellectual nourishment.

M

Make Up: (p.8) May mean you need to make up with someone or even yourself. Can also mean a need or desire to hide who you really are, afraid to face the truth.

Mall: (p.29, 34) Materialism, greed. You may also find yourself in the mall when you need some pampering or are searching for something to make you happy.

Man: Your masculine self, the part of your personality that is assertive, takes action and makes decisions.

Manta Rays: (p.42) Stinging remarks. Something or someone that may seem beautiful but is actually dangerous.

Marriage/Wedding: (p.57, 59, 60) A union of qualities or opinions. Who are you marrying? You need to unite with a quality or opinion of your dream bride or groom until "death do you part.' If marrying an unknown bride or groom then you need to merge the qualities of that gender into your psyche.

Military: (p.77) Time to buckle down, be disciplined and responsible. Could also mean overly disciplined and strict.

Milk: (p.66, 75, 78) Often symbolizes maternal instincts. Do you need to be more nurturing right now? Could also mean you need more calcium in your diet.

Mirror: (p.27, 102) Shows you your true self, how you really appear to others. Like a mirror, our dreams reflect our true selves.

Missing: (p.25, 27) Some part of your personality is missing because you aren't acknowledging it or are afraid to use it. Missing a bus, plane, etc. indicates a fear of missing out on opportunity.

Mother: (p.25, 38, 42, 43, 58, 61, 62, 78) Part of the self that knows what's best. Pay attention to the advice Mom gives in your dream. Your own maternal instincts.

Mountain: (p.21, 33, 83) Can symbolize a goal, an obstacle or even your life. You always want to find yourself on the mountaintop or climbing towards the top as that means progression and success. Can also symbolize spiritual heights.

Mouth: (p.26, 27, 83) Any dream having to do with the mouth points to verbal communication. Take a good look at the things you say, have said or need to say.

Movie: (p.102) This is your life. A projection of your true attitudes, behaviors, etc. Get the picture. May mean more action, less observation.

Murder: (p.87) A need or desire to kill off, to end, something in your life.

N

Naked: (p.13, 14, 16, 17) Feeling vulnerable, exposed, embarrassed. Unprepared to cope with a particular situation. Reveal the truth. Get down to the bare facts.

News/News Anchor/News Paper: (p.70, 71) Information you need to know concerning your personal world.

Nun: (p.16) Your prudish self. Could also be your pure spiritual self, depending on content of dream. May mean the issue is black and white.

O

Ocean/Sea: (p.4, 5, 42, 43) Life giving energy. Emotional depths. Spiritual depths. Creative depths. There are plenty of fish in the sea, much opportunity.

Office: (p.44) May point to a work related issue. You need to work harder at something.

Old Man/Old Woman: (p.102) Passage of time. Old, out dated attitudes and beliefs. Wiser, older self.

Oven: (p.55) Things are heating up! Cooking up ideas and schemes. Also a common symbol for the womb.

P

Party: (p.14) Cause for celebration, reward for a job well done.

Path: (p.70) A path you have chosen to take in life. The condition of the path reflects the ease or the difficulty this path in life has been for you.

Penis: (p.30) Masculine energy. Time to stand up (hee hee) and be assertive.

Phone/Phone Call: (p.46, 47, 96, 97) Lines of communication. May be telling you to say what you need to say and/or listen to what needs to be said.

Pickle: (p.4, 5, 68) Pun for "In a pickle," meaning in a tough situation. A pickle is also preserved, could indicate a need or desire to preserve something.

Pictures/Photos: (p.51, 69) How you picture yourself or a particular situation. Could be your dream saying, "Get the picture?!" Picture this.

Pig: (p.39) Rude and boorish behavior, selfishness.

Pillow: (p.15) A need to be comforted or a need to rest and relax. Pillow talk.

Planting: (p.54) Making the necessary steps for growth. Planting the seed, giving tidbits of information.

Play Room/Play Ground: (p.65) Time to play, have fun with your life, with your choices. May be telling you there is room to play around with a certain decision, project, etc.

Pocket: (p.21) Security, safe keeping, concealing.

Pond: (p.22) Creative juices contained within the mind. Always good to have thriving fish and other critters in your dream pond. Can also mean quiet reflection.

Pool: (p.16, 14, 42) Your emotional pool. Your contained emotions. Could even symbolize something you may want to dive into.

Pregnant: (p.66) About to give birth to something new in your life, something that needs lots of care and attention in order to reach its full potential.

President: (p.68) Your authoritative, decision making self. The part of your personality that presides over your affairs.

Puddle: (p.81, 82) Small body of water formed by rain, which symbolizes tears. Remnants of an emotional situation. Could be telling you to make a splash.

Punishment: (p.9) Usually caused by guilt. Are you punishing yourself?

Purse/Wallet: (p.19, 74) Your identity! We keep our IDs, credit cards and money inside so it symbolizes the credit and value we give ourselves. To lose a purse or wallet indicates a loss of who we are or a loss of credibility.

Pursuer: (p. 7, 52) Symbolizes something or someone you are trying to avoid, an issue you are running from.

Q

Queen: (p.69) Leadership abilities, your ruling feminine qualities.

R

Rain: (p.45, 77) An emotional downpour, tears, sorrow. Rain is a cleansing element so it may be time for a good emotional cleansing.

Recliner: (p.52, 53) Are you being too lazy? Could also mean a need to relax, kick up your feet, stay a while.

Refrigerator: (p.53) Cold feelings. Indicates you have put something in cold storage.

Rhinoceros: (p.39) Thick skinned. Toughen up.

River: (p.44, 60) The flow of life. Go with the flow. Don't fight the current. If trying to cross the river it would indicate that you are trying to cross over into a new area of your life. Is your crossing easy or difficult?

Road: (p.83) The road of life. The type of road and condition of the road will reflect how your journey is going right now.

Road Side: (p.87, 88) Side tracked. Off the beaten path. Non conformity.

Robes: (p.37, 101) Wisdom, enlightenment. A bathrobe would symbolize a recent cleansing or relaxation.

Roller Coaster: (p.94) Symbolizes life, it's full of ups and downs. Emotions. Could reflect a particular situation. Going along for the ride.

Rooms: (p.22, 50) Each different room reflects a different aspect of the self. What is that particular room used for? Finding new rooms indicates discovery of new elements to your personality.

Roots: (p.27) Family from whence you came. Getting to the source of the issue. Secure grounding. May indicate you need to dig deeper.

Ruins: (p.70) Your past. Are you rediscovering yourself?

Running: (p.8) Do you need to pick up the pace somewhere in your life? Are you trying to keep up? Things may be going too fast. Slow down. If you are running from something then you are probably avoiding something or someone in your waking life.

S

School: (p.14, 25, 46) Time to learn a lesson or educate yourself on certain matters. You may be feeling tested or that you need to pass a particular situation with flying colors. Do you have a fear of failure? If searching for a class you are directionless in some area of your life. If you are late for class you are afraid of missing an opportunity or are feeling unprepared.

Searching: (p.20, 21,74) Feeling directionless, hopeless. Time to go inward and search within yourself.

Sex: (p.57, 60, 67) A union of qualities or opinions. Pick three words that describe your dream lover. Apply those words to yourself, to your life. Would you or your life improve if you took on one of those qualities or opinions?

Shadow: (p.52, 82) Aspect of self that you do not recognize and that you fear. If not acknowledged it will follow you.

Shoes: (p.20) Grounding, footing, standing firm, stability, protection. If you've lost your shoes you may be feeling unsure, unstable.

Shrinking: (p.13) Something is becoming less important or less of an option.

Sick: (p.38, 43) Something in your life is not good for you. You are in need of emotional, spiritual or physical healing.

Sink: (p.81, 82) Place of cleansing. Wash away your negativity. If your sink is clogged then you are holding in negativity.

Skateboarding: (p.35) Skating around the issue. Could also mean accomplishing something with ease.

Skin: (p.88, 89) Your protection of your feelings and ideas. Thick skinned. If something is embedded in your skin then someone or something in waking life is irritating you, getting under your skin.

Skyscraper: (p.9) Something in your life that you have built. Could even symbolize yourself. High aspirations. The sky's the limit.

Slide: Sliding deep down into your subconscious. Time to do some introspection. Can also mean you are accomplishing something with ease.

Smoking: (p.14) Rude offensive. Could symbolize a bad habit. Hot, sexy.

Snake: (p.38) Masculine energy. Healing energy. A fear or temptation, something that could turn into a poisonous situation.

Song/Singing: (p.49, 96, 97) Pay attention to the title and to the lyrics. Do they say anything about your current situation? Singing indicates happiness, harmony.

Soup: (p.38) Can symbolize fellowship. May also symbolize a healing energy. What kind of soup was in your dream? It may give a clue as to what can make thengs in your life better.

Stab: (p.87) Hurtful remarks.

Stairs: (p.13, 44, 65, 67, 84, 91) Progression or digression depending on which way you are going. You always want ta find yourself going up, on to the next level.

Sting: (p. 42) Hurtful words

Stickman: (p.58) Basic, simple, uncomplicated. It's a black and white issue.

Stomach: (p.28) Your gut instincts. Sick to your stomach. Place where you process information.

Store: (p.16, 17) Your inner storehouse of ideas, attitudes, resourcefulness, always at your disposal.

Storm: (p.22, 44) A stormy situation. An emotional outburst. Anger.

Stranger: (p.60) Part of your personality you are unfamiliar with. Time to become familiar with this aspect of yourself.

Stripping: (p.15, 88, 89) Reveal the truth. Strip away old or negative attitudes.

Surgery: (p.28, 29) You may need to remove something from your life. Something in your life or within you needs reparation.

Swing: (p.50) Swinging back and forth on a decision. You may be acting childish.

T

Tail: (p.62, 63) Your past. Something you should leave behind you. May also indicate you or someone around you is lying, telling a tale.

Teeth: (p.26) Most often symbolizes your words. If teeth are falling out then you have been having loose speech, speaking without thinking or gossiping. If you are spitting out your teeth then there is something that needs to be said.

Toes: (p.28, 29) Get a grip. Standing firm.

Toilet: (p.41) Your ability to release and flush away negativity. If toilet is clogged or filthy then you are not processing your negativity well, you are holding things in.

Tongue: (p.26, 27) Verbalization. Look at what you have recently said or need to say.

Topless: (p.16) A need or desire to reveal your feelings.

Traffic: (p.10, 19, 87, 88) Symbolizes the pace of your life. Is your traffic moving smoothly? Is it too fast? Is it at a standstill?

Trapped: (p.16) Lack of movement in your life. Are you stuck in a situation you don't know how to get out of? How have you contributed to your imprisonment?

Tree: (p.45) Family. Branching out. Going back to your roots. Aiming high while remaining grounded and down to earth.

Truck: (p.9) Your vehicle through life or a particular situation. Most often associated with work. Your ability to carry a heavy burden.

Turtles: (p.75, 76) Slow going. Be patient. Also a common symbol in pregnant women's dreams, symbolizes the fetus.

U

UFO: (p.50) Something unfamiliar to you. Can also symbolize a higher awareness.

V

Vines: (p.43, 73) Growth, the family line. Can also symbolize a clinging person or issue.

Vomit: (p.38) Something in your life is not good for you. An urgent need to release negativity.

W

Wake Up: (p.34) You need to wake up and pay attention to a particular issue in your life.

Wall: (p.43, 52) An obstacle or barrier you have built yourself. Protection.

Water: (p.41, 42, 43, 44, 45, 46, 70, 71) Your emotions. The state of the water will reflect the state of your emotions. Can also symbolize creative juices. A healing energy.
    Clear Water: Clear about emotional decisions
    Muddy, Murky Water: Emotional confusion. Unable to see through an emotional issue. Depression.
    Rising Water/Flood: You may be getting in over your head, getting in too deep. An increasingly tough situation.
    Under Water: In over your head. Feeling overwhelmed

Whale: (p.33, 39) A whale of an issue. A whale of an accomplishment.

Window: (p.43, 93, 94, 102) Your perception of things. Ability to see through a barrier.

Woman: (p.39, 61, 63) Feminine aspects of your personality, creativity, sensitivity, ability to nurture, passiveness.

Worm: (p.30, 78) Something may be bugging you. Has someone or something wormed its way into your life? A low opinion of yourself.

Wrist: (p.30) Flexibility

Wrong Turn: Unplanned turn of events. Bad decision.

Wizard/Magician: (52, 53) Your ability to create anything you want for yourself

Z

Zombie: (p.81) Something that you thought was gone but is trying to come back to life. No longer in touch with feelings or reality. Unemotional.